VISUALIZING
THE UNKNOWN BALKANS

VIZUALIZACIJA
NEPOZNATOG BALKANA

Cover / Naslovnica: Northern Trench of Svinjarička Čuka / Naslovna strana: Severna sonda na lokalitetu Svinjarička Čuka (photo/fotografija: F. Ostmann)

All rights reserved.
ISBN 978-3-7001-8811-7
Copyright © OREA, Austrian Academy of Sciences, Vienna 2020
Layout: Angela Schwab
Printing: Prime Rate, Budapest
https://epub.oeaw.ac.at/8811-7
https://verlag.oeaw.ac.at
Made in Europe

Table of Contents / Sadržaj

Preface

The idea for this booklet is closely related to the research focus on Balkan archaeology of the OREA Institute of the Austrian Academy of Sciences and its various collaboration partners. Thanks to the financial support of the Innovation Fund of the Austrian Academy of Sciences, it has been possible to realize the *Visualizing the Unknown Balkans* project over the last two years. The present booklet aims to set out a physical paper-based summary accompanying a digital 3D movie produced within the framework of the Innovation Fund project. The fragmentation of modern-day archaeology on the Balkans, its high impact on the European past and its scientific attractiveness constitute our starting point for turning a new spotlight on Balkan archaeology for a broader audience.

Visualizing the complex and multi-level research results of interdisciplinary teams represents one of the challenges in state-of-the-art archaeology these days. In explaining and disseminating the outcome of excavations and fieldwork, we could have realized various initiatives for a scientific and broader public. Open-days for guests and press conferences during the excavations in Bosnia and Herzegovina and in Serbia have attracted lots of media attention since 2018. Our new results have been presented in lectures at the Austrian embassies in Belgrade and Sarajevo as well as in lectures held at several international scientific congresses. Recently excavated objects and finds from Svinjarička Čuka (Serbia) were presented in an exhibition and its accompanying catalogue at the Schallaburg in Lower Austria in 2020.

Implementing this multi-level visualization approach was only possible due to the engaged support of many institutions. We are thankful to all the Serbian authorities, especially the Serbian Ministry of Culture and Heritage and our collaboration partners at the Institute of Archaeology in Belgrade. The Ministry for Education, Science, Culture and Sport of the Zenica-Doboj Canton supported our investigations in Bosnia and Herzegovina. We would also like to thank the Armed Forces of Bosnia and Herzegovina for providing help during the excavation in Bijeljina. We additionally thank the National Museum in Leskovac, the Museum of Mining and Metallurgy in Bor, the Museum of Semberija in Bijeljina and the Museum of the City of Zenica. We would like to express our sincere thanks to the Austrian Embassy in Belgrade, the ambassador Nikolaus Lutterotti and Sabine Kroissenbrunner as well as to the cultural attaché Adrien Feix and the first secretary of the Austrian Embassy in Sarajevo, Nicola Hardwick.

The results presented here are based on ongoing research fieldwork in the Balkans, funded by the Austrian Science Fund (FWF projects no. P32096-G25 and no. P32095-G25). We especially thank the Austrian Academy of Sciences and its Innovation Fund for supporting our initiative. We would like to thank the Austrian Academy of Sciences Press for supporting this publication, Angela Schwab for the layout of the present booklet, Irene Petschko for its organization, Felix Ostmann for the help with images/photos and Nicola Wood for the English editing. Finally, we thank each and every member of our excavation teams and all authors for sharing their expertise with us, namely Snježana Antić, Michael Brandl, Aleksandar Bulatović, Clare Burke, Aleksandar Kapuran, Bogdana Milić, Mathias Mehofer, Ognjen Đ. Mladenović, Irene M. Petschko and Lukas Waltenberger (in alphabetical order).

We hope that the present booklet supports the Visualizing of the Unknown Balkans, revives further interest and informs a broader audience about the continued attractiveness of Balkan archaeology!

Vienna, 8.7.2020

Mario Gavranović / Barbara Horejs

Predgovor

Ideja za izradu ove brošure usko je povezana sa istraživačkim fokusom na balkansku arheologiju OREA Instituta Austrijske akademije nauka i raznih partnera. Realizacija projekta „Vizualizacija nepoznatog Balkana" u protekle dvije godina omogućena je zahvaljujući finansijskoj podršci Fonda za inovacije Austrijske akademije nauka. Ova brošura, pored digitalnog 3D filma, ima za cilj da prikaže sažetak istraživanja sprovedenih u okviru projekta. Fragmentacija moderne arheologije na Balkanu, njen veliki utjecaj na evropsku prošlost kao i njena atraktivnost sa naučnog stanovišta polazne su tačke novog interesa za balkansku arheologiju i njenog predstavljanja široj publici.

Vizualizacija složenih i primjenom različitih metoda dobivenih rezultata istraživanja od strane interdisciplinarnih timova predstavlja jedan od velikih izazova savremene arheologije. Prezentacija i popularizacija rezultata terenskog rada i arheoloških iskopavanja u okviru projekta pokrenula je niz raznih javnih inicijativa usmjerenih ka široj i naučnoj javnosti. Otvoreni dani za goste i konferencije za štampu tokom naših istraživanja u Bosni i Hercegovini i Srbiji izazvali su zavidnu medijsku pažnju. Rezultati projekta predstavljeni su na predavanjima u austrijskim ambasadama u Beogradu i Sarajevu, kao i na nekoliko međunarodnih naučnih skupova. Nedavno otkriveni predmeti i nalazi sa iskopavanja na Svinjaričkoj Čuki (Srbija) predstavljeni su 2020 na izložbi u Schallaburgu u Donjoj Austriji kao i u pratećem katalogu.

Realizacija kompleksnog projekta vizualizacije arheoloških istraživanja omogućena je zahvaljući angažiranoj podršci mnogih institucija. Zahvaljujemo se vlastima u Republici Srbiji , posebno Ministarstvu kulture i baštine Republike Srbije i našim partnerima sa Arheološkog instituta u Beogradu. Ministarstvo za obrazovanje, nauku, kulturu i sport Zeničko-dobojskog kantona podržalo je naše istraživanje u Bosni i Hercegovini. Takođe se zahvaljujemo Oružanim snagama Bosne i Hercegovine na pružanju pomoći tokom iskopavanja u Bijeljini. Dodatno se zahvaljujemo Narodnom muzeju u Leskovcu, Muzeju rudarstva i metalurgije u Boru, Muzeju Semberije u Bijeljini i Muzeju grada Zenice. Iskreno se zahvaljujemo austrijskoj ambasadi u Beogradu, ambasadorima Nikolaus Lutterotti i Sabine Kroissenbrunner, atašeu za kulturu Adrienu Feixu i prvoj sekretarici austrijske ambasade u Sarajevu Nicoli Hardwick.

Predstavljeni rezultati inicirali su nekoliko tekućih terenskih istraživanja na Balkanu koje finansira Austrijski naučni fond (FWF projekti br. P32096-G25 i br. P32095-G25). Posebno se zahvaljujemo Austrijskoj akademiji nauka i Fondu za inovacije koji su podržali našu inicijativu. Željeli bismo da se zahvalimo i medijskom odjeljenju Austrijske akademije nauka koje je podržalo izradu ove publikacije, Angeli Schwab za tehničku izradu i dizajn, Irene Petschko za organizaciju, Felixu Ostmannu za pomoć u odabiru fotografija i Nicoli Wood za redakciju engleskih tekstova. Na kraju se zahvaljujemo timovima sa naših iskopavanja i svim autorima koji su sa nama učestvovali u izradi tekstova, a to su Snježana Antić, Michael Brandl, Aleksandar Bulatović, Clare Burke, Aleksandar Kapuran, Bogdana Milić, Mathias Mehofer, Ognjen Đ. Mladenović, Irene M. Petschko i Lukas Waltenberger (po abecednom redu).

Nadamo se da će ova brošura uspješno predstaviti prve rezultate projekta „Vizualizacija nepoznatog Balkana" i pobuditi dalji interes te ujedno informirati širu publiku o fascinantnoj balkanskoj arheologiji i njenoj neprekidnoj privlačnosti!

Beč, 8.7.2020

Mario Gavranović / Barbara Horejs

INTRODUCTION

UVOD

Mario Gavranović / Barbara Horejs

Bijeljina

Gradišće

Kopilo

Trnjane
Hajdučka Česma
Čoka Njica

Humska Čuka

Bubanj

Svinjarička Čuka

Ranutovac

Sava

Danube

Sava

Great Morava

West Morava

Danube

Bosna

Drina

Vardar

0   50   100
km

Visualizing the Unknown Balkans

The visualization of the archaeological heritage from the Balkans turns the spotlight on the human past in this region that is in many ways essential for our understanding of European history in general. Southeast Europe represents one of the key areas for analysing the human past, where most of the major cultural developments started that had a long-lasting impact on the continent. This specific culmination of cultural and social dynamics over millennia took place in the highly diverse, but connected landscapes of the Balkans. These distinct characteristics form the backbone of one of the most exciting and challenging areas for archaeology on the globe. The Austrian Academy of Sciences has a long-standing research tradition in southeastern Europe, with the OREA Institute supporting prehistoric archaeology in close cooperation with partners in several countries on the Balkans.

Booklet and Digital Movie

Visualizing the Unknown Balkans offers an overview of ongoing interdisciplinary fieldwork in Bosnia and Herzegovina and in Serbia covering a time span of about six millennia. The results, in the form of maps, plans, geophysical screenings and digital reconstructions, open up new perspectives for potential future investigations and set the course for the broader public and scientific perception of archaeological research in the region. Virtual archaeological heritage datasets are created for potential citizen science participation, for use in local museums as well as for scientists interested in Balkan archaeology. The present booklet accompanies a digital 3D movie offering a multi-dimensional impression of the scientific results (which can be found online on the project website: https://vub.orea.oeaw.ac.at/). More details on our research are available via our scientific publications, listed in a bibliography at the end of this booklet.

Case Studies

Altogether five case studies are presented in this overview, located in different micro-regions of the central and western Balkans. The interdisciplinary results provide a good starting point for digital reconstruction of the diverse prehistoric landscapes and the distinct societies living in these areas at different times.

Area 1 (*First farmers and herders in south Serbia*) is located in southern Serbia with the site of Svinjarička Čuka representing the Neolithic period of early farming communities. The site was newly identified by an Austro-Serbian team and excavations have been undertaken within this cooperation since 2018.

Area 2 (*The rising of Copper Age central places*) in the South Morava Valley with the site of Velika Humska Čuka is being excavated by the Institute of Archaeology in Belgrade and the National Museum in Niš and represents the Copper Age in the present booklet.

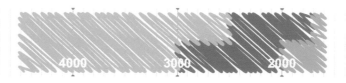

6000   4000   3000   2000   1000

Area 3 (Bronze Age metallurgy in east Serbia) is situated in eastern Serbia near the industrial metal centre of Bor and includes the joint Austro-Serbian investigations of the Bronze Age settlements Trnjane and Čoka Njica with clear traces of metallurgical activities and copper ore smelting, as well as excavations in the recently discovered necropolis of Hajdučka Česma with urns in the cremation graves.

Area 4 (Bronze Age communities in central Bosnia) is located in the Zenica Basin in central Bosnia, investigated by an Austro-Bosnian team since 2019, and includes three sites. Gradišće represents Bronze Age burial places in the Dinaric Alps. The hillfort of Kopilo is located on the opposite side of the Bosna River and had a long continuity of occupation between the Late Bronze Age and the end of the Iron Age.

Area 5 (Prehistoric burial mounds (tumuli) in northeastern Bosnia) covers the research into prehistoric burial mounds near the city of Bijeljina (Republic of Srpska) in the plainlands of northeastern Bosnia-Herzegovina. The impressive monuments in Novo Selo and Muharine were previously unknown in the archaeological literature. The intensive prospection and subsequent excavation revealed the use of these sites as burial grounds during the Copper and Bronze Ages and in the Middle Ages.

Vizualizacija nepoznatog Balkana

Vizualizacija arheološke baštine Balkana i proučavanje ljudske prošlosti na ovim prostorima u mnogo čemu su ključni za razumjevanje evropske istorije u cjelini. Jugoistočna Evropa jedno je od najvažnijih arheoloških područja, odakle je započeo veliki broj kulturnih strujanja koja su imala dugotrajan utjecaj na kontinent. Specifičan kulturni i društveni razvoj odigrao se u vrlo raznolikim ali međusobno povezanim predjelima tokom više milenija. Ovaj skup posebnih karakteristika čini Balkan jednim od najuzbudljivijih i najizazovnijih područja na svijetu kada je riječ o arheologiji. Istraživanja na prostoru jugoistočne Evrope dio su duge naučne tradicije Austrijske akademija nauka, a posebno težište na prahistorijsku arheologiju inicirao je institut OREA u saradnji sa partnerima iz nekoliko zemalja.

Brošura i film

„Vizualizacija nepoznatog Balkana" nudi pregled interdisciplinarnih terenskih radova u Bosni i Hercegovini i Srbiji na nalazištima koja pokrivaju vremenski period od oko šest milenija. Rezultati u obliku geografskih karata, planova, geofizičkih prospekcija i digitalnih rekonstrukcija otvaraju nove perspektive za potencijalna buduća istraživanja te doprinose široj javnoj i naučnoj percepciji arheoloških istraživanja. Virtuelne predstave arheološke baštine kreirane su za potencijalno učešće šire javnosti i mogu koristiti kako lokalnim muzejima tako i naučnicima koje zanima balkanska arheologija. Ovu brošuru prati digitalni 3D film koji nudi višedimenzionalnu predstavu naučnih rezultata (koji se mogu naći online na veb

stranici projekta: vub.orea.oeaw.ac.at). Više detalja o istraživanju dostupno je i putem stručnih publikacija koje su navedene u bibliografiji.

Regionalne studije

U ovom pregledu ukupno je predstavljeno pet studija koje se nalaze u različitim mikro-regijama centralnog i zapadnog Balkana. Interdisciplinarnim pristupom dobiveni su prvi rezultati koji čine dobru polaznu tačku za digitalnu rekonstrukciju raznolikih praistorijskih pejzaža i karakterističnih prahistorijskih društava koja su na tim prostorima živjela.

Regija 1 (Prvi zemljoradnici i stočari u južnoj Srbiji) prati razvoj ranih poljoprivrednih zajednica na jugu Srbije istraživanjem na neolitskom nalazištu Svinjarička Čuka. Ovaj lokalitet nedavno je identifikovao austrijsko-srpski a u okviru saradnje iskopavanja se obavljaju od 2018.

Regija 2 (Uspon centralnih mesta bakarnog doba) u dolini Južne Morave sa lokalitetom Velika Humska Čuka istražuje se od strane Arheološkog instituta u Beogradu i Narodnog muzeja u Nišu i predstavlja bakarno doba u ovoj brošuri.

Regija 3 (Metalurgija bronzanog doba u istočnoj Srbiji) nalazi se u istočnoj Srbiji u blizini rudarsko-metalurškog centra Bor i obuhvata zajednička austrijsko-srpska istraživanja na više lokaliteta. U naseljima Trnjane i Čoka Njica pronađeni su jasni tragovi metalurških aktivnosti i topljenja bakarne rude iz bronzanog doba a iz istog perioda potiče i nekropola Hajdučka česma sa grobovima u urnama.

Regija 4 (Zajednice bronzanog doba u centralnoj Bosni) nalazi se u bazenu rijeke Bosne u blizini Zenice u centralnoj Bosni. Istraživanja od strane austrijsko-bosanskog tima traju od 2018. godine i uključujuviše lokaliteta . Gradišće predstavlja specifičan kompleks više naselja i grobnih mjesta iz bronzanog doba u planinskom prostoru Dinarskog masiva. Utvrđeno visinsko naselje Kopilo nalazi se na suprotnoj strani rijeke Bosne sa izrazitim kontinuitetom naseljavanja između kasnog bronzanog i kraja željeznog doba.

Regija 5 (Praistorijski grobovi [tumuli] u sjeveroistočnoj Bosni) pokriva istraživanje praistorijskih tumula u ravničarskom prostoru sjeveroistočne Bosne i Hercegovine u blizini grada Bijeljine (Republika Srpska). Impresivni grobni spomenici u Novom Selu i Muharinama bili su dosad nepoznati u arheološkoj literaturi. Intenzivne prospekcije i iskopavanja otkrili su kako su ova mjesta korištena kao groblja tokom bakarnog i bronzanog doba te u srednjem vijeku.

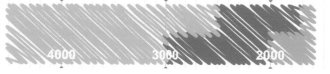

FIRST FARMERS AND HERDERS IN SOUTH SERBIA

PRVI ZEMLJORADNICI I STOČARI U JUŽNOJ SRBIJI

Barbara Horejs / Michael Brandl / Bogdana Milić / Clare Burke

Sava

Danube

Great Morava

West Morava

South Morava

Nišava

Svinjarička Čuka

Vardar

0   50
km

First Farmers and Herders in South Serbia

The Beginnings of the Neolithic in the Central Balkans

The transformation from mobile hunter-gatherers into permanent living farmers and herders took place around 6000 calBC in the area of the central Balkans up to the Danube Gorges. The new period of the Neolithic is archaeologically associated with the so-called Starčevo horizon, named after the famous site close to Belgrade on the Danube's left bank. The new way of subsistence and innovative technologies are related to migrations from Anatolia and the Aegean into the Balkans, as recently also demonstrated by aDNA studies of human remains. The genetic relations between farming communities in the Danube region and Anatolia allow us to assume small-scale movements of people along different routes, of which the South and Great Morava River valleys seem highly important in connecting the Aegean Sea via the Axios-Vardar-Morava route with the Danube and the Pannonian Plain.

Prvi zemljoradnici i stočari u Južnoj Srbiji

Počeci neolita na centralnom Balkanu

Na području centralnog Balkana, sve do Đerdapa, transformacija od lovačko-sakupljačkih zajednica ka društvima zemljoradnika i stočara odigrala se oko 6000 pre nove ere. Taj novi period – neolit – arheološki se dovodi u vezu sa takozvanim starčevačkim horizontom, koji ime nosi prema po čuvenom lokalitetu na levoj obali Dunava, nedaleko od Beograda. Novi način opstanka i inovativne tehnologije koje su obeležile ovaj period vezuju se za migracije iz Anatolije i Egeje na Balkan, na šta su nedavno ukazale i studije drevne DNK na ljudskim ostacima. Genetske veze između zemljoradničkih zajednica Podunavlja i Anatolije sugerišu različite puteve kretanja manjih grupa ljudi, a čini da su prostori uz Južnu i Veliku Moravu odigrali izuzetno važnu ulogu u povezivanju Egejske obale sa Dunavom i Panonskom nizijom, posredstvom rečnih dolina Vardara i Morave.

Still Unknown in the Central Balkans

However, we are lacking any excavated early Neolithic sites, particularly along the South Morava route, to enable us to understand not only the beginnings of this crucial step in humankind, but also the process of its intensification during the following generations. When did farming become the main component in humans' subsistence strategy? How did the communities change after establishing permanent villages and living together with their livestock? How long did it take to create the "cultural landscape" within the co-evolutionary process of human and environment interaction? How did communities manage the natural resources, establish new ways of exchange and create far-reaching networks? Why are some innovative technologies successful and have consequently been widely adopted, whereas others have not been transmitted further into the European continent? Overall, which social and cultural impacts can be linked with these fundamental economic and ecological changes, which shaped European societies for the following millennia? Modern archaeology aims to shed light on these questions by applying a variety of scientific disciplines for studying the remains of prehistoric societies in their distinct contexts.

Još uvek "nepoznato" na centralnom Balkanu

Uprkos velikom značaju centralnog Balkana za proces neolitizacije, vidljiv je nedostatak ranoneolitskih lokaliteta koji bi nam pomogli ne samo u razumevanju ovog ključnog koraka u prošlosti čovečanstva već i njegovog intenzivnog razvoja tokom narednih generacija, naročito u dolini Južne Morave. Kada je poljoprivreda postala ključna komponenta u ljudskim strategijama preživljavanja i opstanka? Kakve su promene doživele ljudske zajednice nakon osnivanja stalnih naselja i kako je zavisnost od proizvodnje hrane uticala na njihove živote? Koliko je vremena bilo potrebno za formiranje „kulturnog pejzaža" u okviru koevolutivnog procesa interakcije ljudi i njihove okoline? Kako su ljudske zajednice raspolagale prirodnim resursima, uspostavile nove načine razmene i ostvarile veze sa udaljenim zajednicama? Zašto su neke od novih tehnologija bile uspešne i kao takve postale opšteprihvaćene, dok neke druge nisu našle svoj put na evropski kontinent? Konačno, da li se i koji društveni i kulturni uticaji mogu povezati sa takvim fundamentalnim ekonomskim i ekološkim promenama, koje su oblikovale evropska društva u narednim milenijumima? Moderna arheologija ima za cilj da rasvetli ova pitanja kroz različite naučne discipline, proučavajući ostatke praistorijskih društava u različitim kontekstima.

Searching for the Neolithic in the Leskovac Basin

The Leskovac area represents the first broader basin along the South Morava River route in southern Serbia, presumably attractive to early farmers seeking for agricultural land. Its low elevations between the tributary rivers to the South Morava seem especially promising in our search for potential Neolithic remains, while the area in the vicinity of the main rivers is still frequently flooded, scarcely settled and does not, at first sight, offer stable conditions. A new Austrian-Serbian project started in 2017 to investigate these areas with geoarchaeological and environmental surveys. Altogether it was possible to identify five potential Neolithic sites, which offer excellent opportunities for new interdisciplinary research. Surface collections of finds were conducted during extensive and intensive archaeological surveys and systematic fieldwalking. With the help of Geographical Information System (GIS) analytical tools, the collected finds have been statistically analysed with regard to their spatial distribution and density. Additional non-destructive geophysical surveys provided geomagnetic data for anomalies underneath the surface indicating distinct human activity remains, such as pits or burnt structures. Prospections by drilling delivered an insight into the sediments, soils and pedology of the landscape as well as into the deposition of past human activities. Preserved burnt micro-remains recorded in the drill cores were sampled and dated using the radiocarbon method (based on the radioactive decay of the carbon isotope C14). All methods together reveal the use of the Leskovac area in Neolithic times starting already c. 8200–8000 years ago.

Potraga za neolitom u Leskovačkom basenu

Područje Leskovca predstavlja prvi širi sliv dolinom Južne Morave na jugu Srbije, i verovatno je predstavljalo privlačnu destinaciju za prve zemljoradnike u njihovoj stalnoj potrazi za plodnim zemljištem. Niži predeli između Morave i njenih pritoka deluju naročito značajni u našoj potrazi za potencijalnim tragovima neolita, jer su doline većih reka i danas plavne, retko naseljene i na prvi pogled ne pružaju pogodne uslove za naseljavanje. Austrijsko-srpski projekat iniciran je 2017. godine sa ciljem da se upravo ova oblast geoarheološki i ekološki detaljno istraži. Tokom projekta identifikovano je pet potencijalnih neolitskih lokaliteta, što je otvorilo različite mogućnosti za realizaciju novih interdisciplinarnih istraživanja. Sakupljanje površinskih nalaza vršeno je tokom opsežnog i intenzivnog arheološkog rekognosciranja i sistematskog obilaska terena. Prikupljeni nalazi statistički su analizirani na osnovu prostorne distribucije i gustine nalaza, upotrebom različitih analitičkih alata poput Geografskog informacionog sistema (GIS). Dodatna nedestruktivna geofizička ispitivanja rezultovala su otkrivanjem različitih anomalija ispod površine zemlje, koje ukazuju na tragove različitih ljudskih aktivnosti kao što su jame i goreli objekti. Paleogeografska bušenja pružila su uvid u sedimente, tipove zemljišta i pedologiju, kao i o naslojavanju tragova ljudskih aktivnosti u prošlosti. Mikro ostaci prikupljeni na ovaj način su uzorkovani i radiokarbonski datovani (datovanje zasnovano na radioaktivnom raspadanju ugljenikovog izotopa C14). Sve gorenavedene metode pružile su nedvosmislene dokaze o naseljavanju Leskovačkog basena tokom ranog neolita, pre oko 8200/8000 godina.

Excavations at Svinjarička Čuka

Archaeological excavations at the newly identified site of Svinjarička Čuka in the Lebane district of southern Serbia were started in 2018 by an Austrian-Serbian team. The site is located on a slightly elevated river terrace next to the famous Caričin Grad, a fortification from the 6th century AD also known as Justiniana Prima. Archaeological and geo-physical surveys in combination with core drilling supported the identification of this new Neolithic site. The excavations recovered remains of human activities from around 7600 years ago. Analysis of these by an interdisciplinary team of experts gave a first insight into the Neolithic societies.

A few recovered structures of pits, ovens, a flat stone feature and a burnt hut built in the wattle and daub technique indicate a Neolithic community living on the river terrace, at least temporarily. This group practised farming of wheat, emmer, einkorn and pulses. Their nutrition with domesticated sheep, goat, pig and cattle was supplemented by the hunted wild species of red deer, wild pig, roe deer, ibex, badger and fox. The Neolithic farmers, herders and hunters produced their own textiles, jewellery and did all characteristic kinds of household-work. Their material remains can be associated with the so-called Starčevo cultural horizon and demonstrate their integration into a broad network of farmers and herders between the Danube and North Macedonia. Future excavations are expected to recover older layers situated underneath to provide data on the first generations of the farming pioneers in southern Serbia.

The Neolithic community of the Svinjarička River terrace was very experienced in the management of the available resources, of which workable stones and minerals are of special importance in the Stone Age. The accessibility of good-quality resources in the direct vicinity of the site might be one reason for the first pioneers occupying this region around 8000 years ago. Another important aspect is represented in the fruitful environment, which presumably offered a suitable landscape for early agriculture in appropriate conditions. Both elements – raw material sources and environmental conditions – are key for understanding the establishment of first farming communities and permanent villages within a new area. So far, when and how the fundamental new way of life started, developed and became established in the South Morava Valley, as one of the main corridors in the Neolithization of the Balkans, remains as open question

Arheološka istraživanja na lokalitetu Svinjarička Čuka

Sistematska arheološka istraživanja novootkrivenog lokaliteta Svinjarička Čuka u opštini Lebane na jugu Srbije, realizovana od strane austrijsko-srpskog tima stručnjaka, započeta su 2018. godine. Lokalitet se nalazi na blago uzvišenoj rečnoj terasi nedaleko od čuvenog Caričinog Grada, utvrđenja iz 6. veka nove ere, poznatog i kao Justiniana Prima. Lokalitet je registrovan kombinacijom sistematskih arheoloških i geofizičkih rekognosciranja i sondažnih paleogeografskih bušenja. Arheološkim istraživanjima otkriveni su ostaci ljudskih aktivnosti od pre oko 7600 godina. Analizom tih aktivnosti, interdisciplinarni tim stručnjaka ponudio je prvi uvid u život neolitskih zajednica na ovom prostoru.

Nekoliko otkrivenih jama, peći i objekata sačinjenih od ravnih komada kamena, kao i ostaci izgorele kuće koja je izrađena u tehnici pletera i lepa, ukazuju na postojanje neolitske zajednice koja je privremeno naseljavala ovu rečnu terasu. Ta zajednica se bavila uzgojem različitih vrsta pšenica i mahunarki, a ishrana im se pre svega zasnivala na domaćim životinjama (ovce, koze, svinje i goveče), ali i divljim vrstama koje su lovili, poput jelena, divlje svinje, srne, kozoroga, jazavca i lisice. Neolitski zemljoradnici, stočari i lovci proizvodili su tkanine i nakit i obavljali sve svakodnevne kućne poslove. Njihovi materijalni ostaci mogu se dovesti u vezu sa takozvanim starčevačkim kulturnim horizontom, i svedoče o njihovoj integraciji u širu mrežu na prostoru između Dunava i Severne Makedonije. Očekuje se da buduća istraživanja dovedu do otkrića starijih slojeva, koji bi pružili podatke o naseljavanju prvih generacija zemljoradnika na jugu Srbije.

Raw Materials for Stone Tools

Svinjarička Čuka is situated on a particularly advantageous settlement location, rich in water, arable land and another valuable resource: raw materials for chipped stone production. While the former two are widely available within the Pusta Reka region, the latter is rare, especially with regard to quality and abundance.

These requirements are met perfectly in Svinjarička Čuka. Here, a large variety of lithic materials can be collected from river gravels and, additionally, cropping out close to the surface. Geo-archaeological surveys revealed jasper, chalcedony and chert as the main raw materials suitable for stone tool manufacture around Svinjarička Čuka, where they were readily available for the Neolithic settlers. Provenance studies of stone tools were conducted using a combination of macroscopic grouping, microscopic examination (e.g. of characteristic fossil remains), and trace element analyses. Such investigations reveal the exchange networks, intercultural relations, contact spheres and specific traditions of early farming communities. For Svinjarička Čuka, first results indicate a heavily localized pattern of lithic production during the advanced stages of Starčevo between 5600 and 5400 BC. The Neolithic flint knappers relied almost exclusively on cherts of high quality, which originated from the immediate vicinity of the site. By contrast, other materials were only occasionally used. Although underrepresented, the presence of specific raw materials coming from further away indicates that Svinjarička Čuka was also embedded in larger socio-economic networks in the Neolithic central Balkans. This aspect will be one of the focal points of future investigations at this key site for studying the Neolithization of the region.

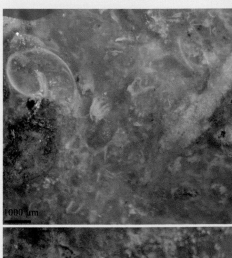

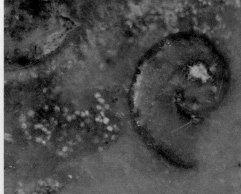

1000 μm

1000 μm

Neolitska zajednica koja je naseljavala terasu Svinjaričke reke imala je iskustva u upravljanju raspoloživim resursima, posebno pogodnim tipovima stena i minerala koji su bili od presudnog značaja tokom kamenog doba. Pristupačna ležišta kvalitetnih sirovina, koja se nalaze u neposrednoj blizini samog lokaliteta, možda su jedan od glavnih razloga za njihovo naseljavanje u ovom kraju pre oko 8000 godina. Još jedan od važnih aspekata prilikom odabira igralo je i plodno okruženje, koje je pružalo pogodne uslove za obrađivanje zemlje. Oba aspekta – dostupnost sirovina i povoljni prirodni uslovi, ključni su za razumevanje procesa osnivanja prvih stalnih naselja na ovom prostoru. Pitanja *kada* i *kako* započinje ovaj fundamentalno novi način života, kako se on formirao i razvijao u dolini Južne Morave kao jednom od glavnih koridora neolitizacije Balkana, ostaju za sada otvorena.

Kamene sirovine

Lokalitet Svinjarička Čuka nalazi se na izuzetno povoljnom položaju koji odlikuju bogata hidrografija, obradivo zemljište i još jedan veoma značajan resurs: kvalitetne sirovine za izradu predmeta od okresanog kamena. Dok su prve dve široko zastupljene u oblasti Puste Reke, poslednja je retka, posebno u pogledu kvaliteta i zastupljenosti.

Lokalitet Svinjarička Čuka ispunjava sve navedene uslove. Raznovrstan litički materijal može se prikupiti iz rečnog šljunka ili sa same površine. Geoarheološka rekognosciranja utvrdila su prisustvo jaspisa, kalcedona i rožnaca pogodnih za izradu kamenih alatki, te su bez sumnje bili lako dostupni stanovnicima neolitskog naselja. Studije porekla sirovine od kojih su kamene alatke bile izrađene realizovane su kombinacijom makroskopskih grupisanja, mikroskopskog ispitivanja (npr. karakteristični fosilni ostaci) i analizom nečistoća. Ovakav pristup omogućava uvid u mreže razmene, međusobne odnose arheoloških kultura, sfere uticaja i samim time karakteristične tradicije ranih zemljoradničkih zajednica. Prvi rezultati sa lokaliteta Svinjarička Čuka ukazuju na lokalno utemeljenu litičku industriju tokom kasnih faza starčevačkog horizonta, između 5600. i 5400. godine pre nove ere. Neolitska proizvodnja kamenih alatki se gotovo isključivo oslanjala na visokokvalitetne rožnace, dostupne u neposrednoj okolini lokaliteta. Nasuprot tome, druge sirovine su se koristile samo izuzetno. Manja zastupljenost određenih nelokalnih sirovina ipak ukazuje na to da su stanovnici lokaliteta Svinjarička Čuka tokom neolita bili uključeni u šire društveno-ekonomske mreže centralnog Balkana, te će upravo taj aspekt biti u fokusu budućih istraživanja, ključnom za proučavanje procesa neolitizacije u ovoj oblasti.

Chipped Stones

Chipped stone assemblages from the Early and Middle Neolithic in the central Balkans bring valuable insights into the agricultural activities related to village lifestyles of the first half of the 6th millennium BC. These mainly concern plant processing and work with animal hide, meat, bone, antler, and other soft and hard materials such as wood. The chipped stone material of Svinjarička Čuka, being particularly abundant on the site, represents a typical Starčevo assemblage, although to some extent the production methods were limited and predetermined by the availability and accessibility of raw materials. This is seen directly in the outcomes, referring to the use of knapping techniques and modification of tools in an opportunistic way, which sometimes lack the "real" Starčevo features. The community mainly used simple methods for breaking stones by applying direct and indirect percussion with hard and soft hammer stones (another rock or antler) in order to obtain flakes and blades. The main toolkits comprised cutting, scraping, piercing, and plant-processing tools, recognized through the particular form of retouch or traces like silica sheen on the tool's edges. In addition, small inserts speak in favour of the use of composite tools, which were utilized by insertion in a handle made of bone or wood. Future analyses aim to reveal whether these were possibly also used for hunting or mainly for plant work, based on the study of microscopic traces. However, the increased variety of tool types and technologies for tool production can be seen with the involvement of exotic rocks and those that were not available locally. Our task now is to see if these new elements appearing at the site are related to a different pattern of use for raw materials which are not local, or if they are the result of a direct exchange of ready-made tools made in a different manner by other communities.

1cm

Neolithic Pottery Types and Technology

The widespread production and use of ceramic containers was a relatively new phenomenon within the Neolithic but this technology and material culture was widely adopted, with similar styles and vessel shapes being found across large areas, indicating the sharing of technological knowledge and new ideas about how to make and use ceramic material culture in daily life. By reconstructing the different ways that pottery was made and used, we can look at the extent to which potters used the local landscape for raw materials, the repertoire of vessel types made within a specific pottery tradition, how traditions developed over time, and how the pottery practices found compare to those at other sites.

The pottery types excavated from Svinjarička Čuka are of the classical Starčevo tradition with an abundance of jars and deep and shallow bowls, probably used for everyday storage and food preparation and consumption.

Proizvodnja kamenih alatki

Repertoar okresanog kamena iz ranog i srednjeg neolita na centralnom Balkanu donosi dragocene uvide u poljoprivredne aktivnosti povezane sa seoskim načinom života u prvoj polovini 6. milenijuma pre nove ere. Ovaj materijal se uglavnom odnosi na procesuiranje biljnih ostataka i obradu životinjske kože, mesa, kosti, roga i drugih mekih i tvrdih materijala, poput drveta. Okresani kamen sa Svinjaričke Čuke, koji je posebno bogat na ovom lokalitetu, predstavlja tipičan starčevački materijal, iako su metode izrade ograničene i određene dostupnošću kamenih sirovina. To se direktno ogleda u načinima i tehnikama okresivanja kao i modifikaciji alata na oportunistički način, pri čemu ponekad nedostaju „prave" karakteristike Starčeva. Zajednica je uglavnom koristila jednostavne načine izrade kamenih alatki primenom direktnog i indirektnog udara tvrdim i mekim čekićem (kamenom ili rogom) kako bi se dobili odbici i sečiva. Osnovni setovi alatki sastojali su se od alata za sečenje, struganje, probijanje i obradu biljaka, prepoznatih po posebnom obliku retuširanja ili tragova poput silikatnog sjaja na ivicama alatki. Pored toga, mali umeci govore u prilog upotrebi kompozitnih alatki koji su se koristili uglavljivanjem u dršku izrađenu od kosti ili drveta. Na osnovu ispitivanja mikroskopskih tragova na alatkama, buduće analize imaju za cilj da otkriju da li su one eventualno korišćene i za lov ili uglavnom za radove sa biljkama (npr. kao srpovi za žetvu). Prisutnost egzotičnih materijala, pored lokalno dostupnih sirovina, ukazuje na povećanu raznovrsnost tipova alatki i tehnologija proizvodnje. Postavlja se pitanje da li su ovi novi elementi koji se pojavljuju na lokalitetu povezani sa drugačijim obrascem upotrebe nelokalnih sirovina, ili su rezultat direktne razmene gotovih alatki proizvedenih od strane drugih zajednica

1cm

Tipovi neolitske keramike i tehnologija

Široko rasprostranjena proizvodnja i upotreba keramičkih posuda bila je relativno nova pojava koja se javlja u okviru neolita. Tehnologija izrade keramičkih posuda široko je usvojena sa sličnim stilovima i oblicima koji se javljaju na velikim geografskim prostorima. Ova činjenica ukazuje na razmenu tehnološkog znanja i novih ideja izrade i korišćenja keramike u svakodnevnom životu. Kroz rekonstrukciju različitih načina proizvodnje može se sagledati u kojoj su meri grnčari koristili lokalne sirovine, kakav je repertoar posuda izrađenih u okviru određene tradicije te kako su se tradicije razvijale tokom vremena i kako je praksa grnčarstva izgledala u poređenju sa drugim lokalitetima.

Tipovi posuda koji su pronađeni na lokalitetu Svinjarička Čuka pripadaju klasičnoj starčevačkoj tradiciji sa obiljem krčaga i dubokih i plitkih zdela, korišćenih za svakodnevno skladištenje, pripremu i konzumiranje hrane.

Ove posude su napravljene pomoću pločica od gline koje su bile naslagane jedna na drugu kako bi formirale posudu, tehnikom štipanja i izvlačenja gline u željeni oblik. Bikonične zdele su bile izrađene u dve polovine, koje su zatim bile

These vessels were made using slabs of clay that were stacked on top of each other to build up the vessel, pinching and pulling the clay into the desired shape. Biconical bowls were made in two halves that were then stuck together around the belly of the vessel where the join is often still visible. We even still have the potter's finger impressions preserved in some vessels!

Macroscopically, we can already see that there is not a wide variation in the types of raw materials potters used but there are big differences in how coarse the vessels are, and in some vessels we can see the remains of organic temper such as chaff or grass. Microscopic analysis will help to identify the specific rocks and clays in the pottery so that we can locate the geological areas that were potentially used for raw materials.

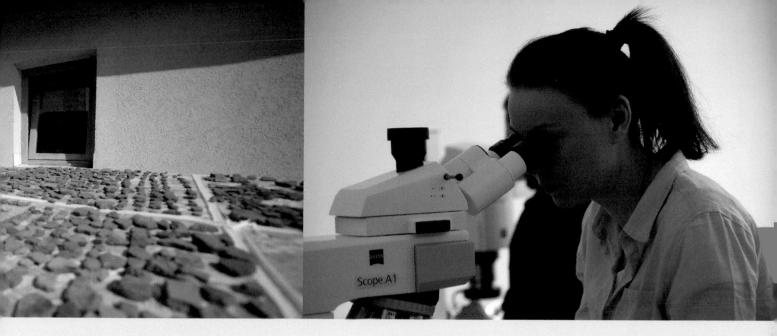

lepljene oko trbuha posude, gde je spoj još uvek često vidljiv . Na nekim posudama još uvek imamo očuvane otiske prstiju grnčara.

Makroskopski je vidljivo da nema velike varijacije u tipovima sirovina koje su grnčari koristili za izradu, već da postoje velike razlike u stepenu obrade površine posuda. Na nekim posudama možemo videti ostatke organskih primesa, kao što su pleva ili trava. Mikroskopska analiza pomoći će da se identifikuju primese u vidu specifičnih stena i glina kako bi se ustanovila geološka područja iz kojih je dobavljana sirovina.

Neolithic Imagery

A characteristic aspect of the prehistoric Balkans is represented in the impressive amounts of imagery produced. The Neolithic communities associated with the Starčevo horizon at Svinjarička Čuka practised a presumably local production of clay figures, symbolizing humans, animals or potentially numinous creatures. This imagery allows an insight into a worldview of early farmers and herders behind the everyday-life practices and subsistence. The human-like (anthropomorphic) and small-sized figures dominate the spectrum of the clay sculptures. The S. Čuka community frequently produced schematic imagery, mostly represented in two types of human-like figurines: female figures with an over-estimated sculpted pelvis and upper legs, a quite schematic body and head without elaborated faces in sitting or standing positions. The sex-related aspects are highly elaborated, mainly with female figures, as demonstrated by the remains of a pregnant woman in a seated position. Male or sex-neutral figures with cylindrical or flat bodies are commonly created with an abstract bird-like face, perhaps imitating a face mask as known from other Vinča-dated sites. Although the figurines' function around 8000 years ago can only be roughly assumed, the variety of imagery points to a potential complex and multi-levelled meaning, reflected in the differences in symbolism of the sex, gender and nature of the creatures illustrated.

Neolitske predstave

Jedan od karakterističnih aspekata praistorije na Balkanu jeste impresivan broj različitih figuralnih predstava. Neolitske zajednice okarakterisane kao nosioci starčevakog horizonta na lokalitetu Svinjarička Čuka verovatno su praktikovale lokalnu proizvodnju glinenih figurina koje simbolišu ljude, životinje ili fantastična (spiritualna) bića. Takve predstave omogućavaju nam uvid u njihovu percepciju sveta, daleko od svakodnevnog života i opstanka. Dominantne su ljudske (antropomorfne) statuete i figurine malih dimenzija. Neolitska zajednica sa lokaliteta Svinjarička Čuka često je izrađivala shematske antropomorfne predstave – ženska figura sa naglašenim kukovima i butinama, figurine šematski prikazanog tela i glave bez naglašenih detalja lica u sedećem ili stojećem položaju. Polne karakteristike su naglašene kod ženskih figurina, što je posebno istaknuto na jednoj od figurina koja predstavlja trudnicu u sedećem položaju. Muške ili polno neutralne figurine sa cilindričnim ili ravnim telima uglavnom su izrađene sa apstraktnim ptičijim licem, koje je možda imitiralo maske koje su poznate sa drugih lokaliteta datovanih u vinčanski period. Iako se funkcija ovih figurina napravljenih pre oko 8000 godina može samo naslutiti, raznolikost predstava ukazuje na moguće postojanje kompleksnih i višeslojnih značenja, koje se ogleda u raznovrsnoj simbolici pola, roda i prirode prikazanih bića.

THE RISING OF COPPER AGE CENTRAL PLACES

USPON CENTRALNIH MESTA BAKARNOG DOBA

Aleksandar Bulatović

The Rising of Copper Age Central Places

Velika Humska Čuka is an archaeological site located in southeastern Serbia, on the northeastern periphery of the village of Hum, approximately 8 km north of the city of Niš. The site is composed of an oval plateau measuring 125 × 150 m. The plateau lies on a dominant elevation (alt. 454.79 m) with steep and inaccessible slopes, except for the northern side of the site that connects it with the opposite elevation known as Mala Humska Čuka.

The site has a visual connection with the eponymous site of Bubanj (8.6 km aerial distance) and the renowned flint outcrop of Kremenac (2.3 km aerial distance). The position of the site dominates the landscape and provides control of most of the Niš Basin. First archaeological excavations of the sites of Velika Humska Čuka and Mala Humska Čuka were conducted in the 1930s and continued on Velika Humska Čuka in the 1950s. The results of those excavations and the excavations at the neighbouring site of Bubanj have provided the basis for the definition of a particular phase of prehistory, marked as the Bubanj-Hum group.

After a long break, archaeological excavations were continued in 2014 by the Institute of Archaeology in Belgrade and the National Museum in Niš. The excavations are still ongoing, with a surface of more than 500 m² examined so far.

Bubanj

Velika Humska
Čuka

Uspon centralnih mesta bakarnog doba

Lokalitet Velika Humska Čuka se nalazi u jugoistočnoj Srbiji, na severoistočnoj periferiji sela Hum, oko 8 km severno od Niša. Čini ga ovalni plato približnih dimenzija 150 × 120 m na vrhu dominantnog uzvišenja (najviša kota 454,79 m) strmih nepristupačnih strana, izuzev severne kojom je ovaj plato povezan sa manjim uzvišenjem poznatim pod nazivom Mala humska čuka.

Lokalitet Velika Humska Čuka je vizuelno povezan sa eponimnim lokalitetom Bubanj (udaljenost vazdušnom linijom 8,6 km), kao i sa čuvenim nalazištem kremena, odnosno opala Kremencem (2,3 km vazdušnom linijom), a sa njega je moguća kontrola većeg dela Niške kotline. Prva arheološka istraživanja lokaliteta Velika Humska Čuka i Mala Humska čuka izvedena su 1930-ih godina, a zatim nastavljena samo na Velikoj humskoj čuki 1950-ih godina, čiji rezultati su, uz rezultate iskopavanja na lokalitetu Bubanj omogućili izdvajanje posebne faze u praistorijskom periodu označene kao bubanjsko-humska grupa.

Posle duže pauze arheološka iskopavanja se nastavljaju 2014. godine u organizaciji Arheološkog instituta u Beogradu i Narodnog muzeja u Nišu, koja traju i danas, tokom kojih je istražena površina od preko 500 m².

Kremenac

Mala Humska Čuka

Cultural layers and enclosed features recorded at the site are attributed to the Early Eneolithic (Bubanj-Hum I, Sălcuța), the Late Eneolithic (Bubanj-Hum II), all phases of the Bronze Age and the Early and Late Iron Age (Late La Tène period). The best-preserved cultural layer belongs to the Early Eneolithic, and it yielded the remains of four houses, multiple kiln floors, and hearths.

Judging by the remains of House 1, which was the best-preserved house at the site, the Early Eneolithic houses had a rectangular ground plan, approximately 5 × 3.5 m in dimension, and were oriented north-south. The houses were built in the wattle and daub technique. A dug-in hearth was recorded in the northern portion of the house, and several ceramic vessels were placed along the axis of the house. The house and its complete inventory were burnt in a large fire.

House 2 was devastated by a large Roman structure, which prevented the precise reconstruction of its ground plan and dimensions. The absolute date for the house puts it into the 44th–43rd century BC. Interestingly, a cooper's chisel weighing 92 g was found in the house, and it represents one of the earliest-dated copper objects in the central Balkans.

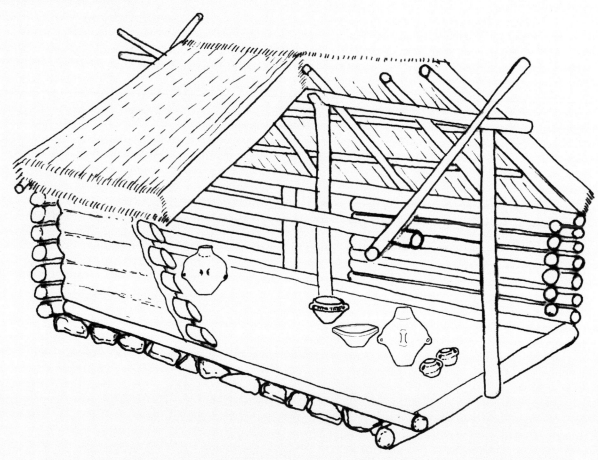

Na lokalitetu su registrovani kulturni slojevi sa zatvorenim celinama iz starijeg eneolita (Bubanj-Hum I, Salcuta IV), poznog eneolita (Bubanj-Hum II), svih faza bronzanog doba, kao i starijeg i mlađeg gvozdenog doba (pozna latenska kultura). Najbolje je očuvan kulturni sloj starijeg eneolita u kojem su evidentirani i istraženi ostaci četiri kuće, kao i više podnica peći, odnosno vatrišta.

Prema ostacima kuće 1, koji su najbolje očuvani, kuće iz ovog perioda su bile pravougaone osnove približnih dimenzija 5 × 3,5 m, orijentacije S-J, izgrađene tehnikom pleteri i lepa. U severnom delu ove kuće nalazilo se ukopano vatrište, a duž ose kuće bilo je poređano nekoliko posuda, koje su zajedno sa kućom izgorele u velikom požaru.

House 3 was damaged by three Roman pits, allowing for only a partial reconstruction of data, such as the wattle and daub technique (fragments of daub decorated with grooves) and several phases of floor renewal, of which the earliest phase is dated to the 45th–44th century BC. Two pits were dug into the younger floor, one of which contained several completely preserved vessels painted in blue, ochre, red, and graphite. Some of the vessels and one large rectangular altar painted in white show evidence of secondary burning. According to the stylistic and typological characteristics, finds from the younger phase of this house are common for the concurrent cultures of the Lower Danube Region, and the most indicative finds from this period are two vessels decorated with a gold coating.

Kuća 2 bila je devastirana velikim rimskim objektom, pa se njen izgled i dimenzije nisu mogli rekonstruisati, a apsolutni datum pokazao je da datira iz 44–43. veka pre n.e. Zanimljivo je da je unutar njenih ostataka nađeno bakarno dleto težine 92 g, koje predstavlja jedan od najstarijih datovanih bakarnih nalaza na centralnom Balkanu.

Kuća 3 bila je oštećena sa tri rimske jame, ali su se neki podaci mogli rekonstruisati, kao što je tip gradnje od pleteri i lepa (sa primercima lepa ukrašenim žlebovima) i više faza obnove podnice, od kojih je najstarija datirala iz 45–44. veka pre n.e. U mlađu podnicu kuće bile su ukopane dve jame, od kojih je u jednoj bilo pohranjeno nekoliko celih posuda oslikanih plavom, belom, oker, crvenom i grafitnom bojom, od kojih su neke sekundarno gorele, kao i jedan veći goreli pravougaoni

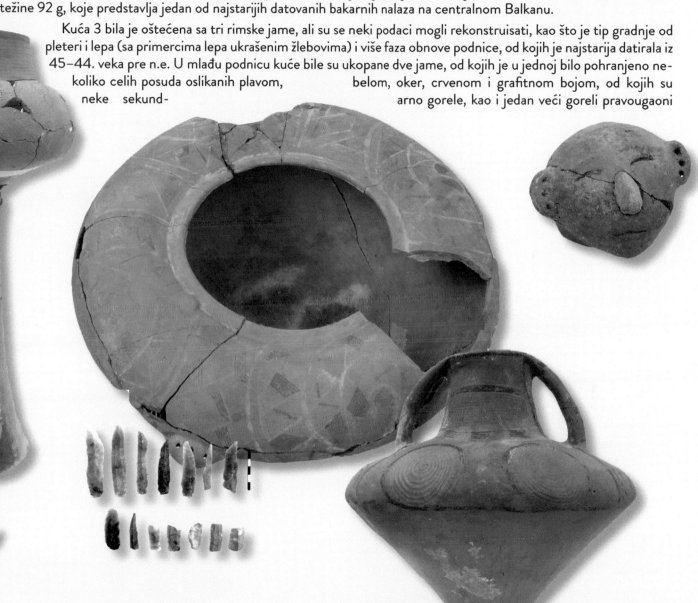

In House 4, excavated in 2019 and dated to a period between the 45th and the 43rd centuries BC, remains of a floor, house inventory, walls made of baked clay decorated with grooves and Early Eneolithic portable finds were all recorded.

Besides the interesting finds from almost all of the prehistoric periods, from the Early Eneolithic to Late La Tène, fragments of red-figure painted pottery from Classical Greece (4th century BC) were also recorded, testifying that the site was inhabited during that period as well. Following the hiatus after the Late La Tène period, the site was last inhabited for a short period during the Late Antique period.

žrtvenik oslikan motivima u beloj boji. Nalazi iz mlađe faze ove kuće, prema stilsko-tipološkim odlikama podsećaju na istovremene kulture iz donjeg Podunavlja, a najindikativniji nalazi iz ovog perioda jesu fragmenti dve posude sa ostacima zlatne prevlake.

U kući 4 otkrivenoj 2019. godine datovanoj u period 45–43. veka pre n.e. registrovani su ostaci podnice, kućnog mobilijara i zidova od pečene zemlje ukrašenih žlebovima, kao i pokretni nalazi iz starijeg eneolita.

Pored interesantnih nalaza iz gotovo svih perioda praistorije od starijeg eneolita do latenskog perioda, na lokalitetu su evidentirani i nalazi slikane crvenofiguralne keramike iz perioda klasične Grčke, odnosno 4. veka pre n.e. koji svedoče da je lokalitet bio nastanjen i u ovom periodu. Nakon hijatusa posle perioda poznog latena lokalitet je bio nakratko nastanjen u kasnoantičkom periodu posle čega se život na njemu potpuno gasi.

PREHISTORIC BURIAL MOUNDS (TUMULI) IN NORTHEASTERN BOSNIA

PRAISTORIJSKE GROBNE HUMKE (TUMULI) U SJEVEROISTOČNOJ BOSNI

Mario Gavranović / Snježana Antić / Lukas Waltenberger

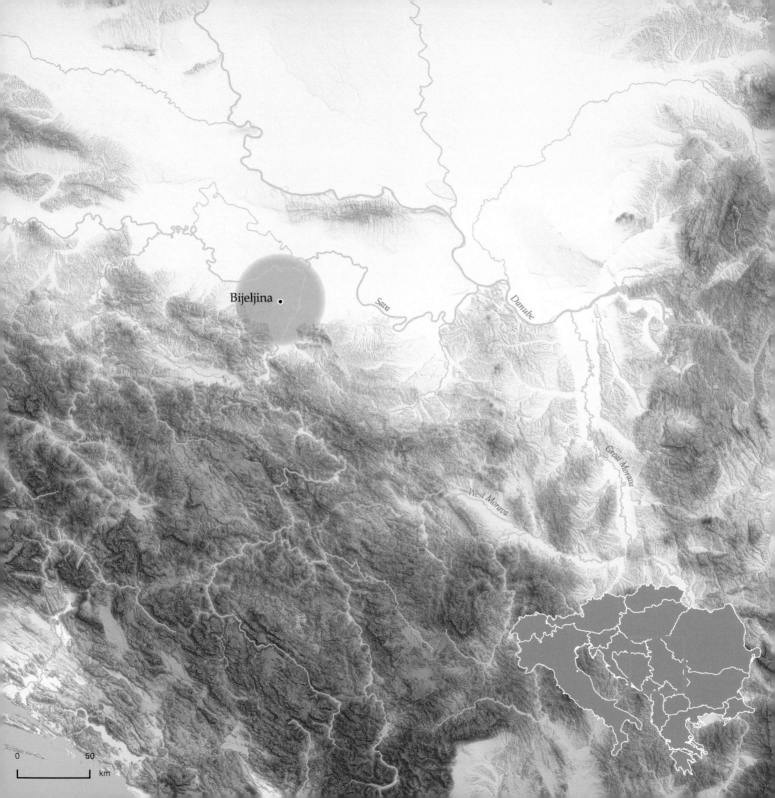

Bijeljina

Sava

Danube

Drina

Bosna

West Morava

Great Morava

0   50
km

Prehistoric Burial Mounds (Tumuli) in Northeastern Bosnia

The large mounds in plains of northeastern Bosnia have thus far remained unregistered in the archaeological literature, despite their prominent position in the immediate vicinity of the city of Bijeljina (Republic of Serbia). Before the start of the research project in a collaboration between the OREA Institute and the Museum of Sembrija in Bijeljina, neither the age nor the interpretation of the earth constructions with a diameter of 40 m in the Novo Selo or Muharine sites could be estimated. The absence of comparable structures and lack of surface finds made it difficult to assess the nature and origins of these impressive human-made monuments. Furthermore, intensive recent agricultural activities led to the flattening and widening of the more or less circular structures so that mounds had a preserved height of 1.5 m.

Position

The investigated and prospected mounds in Novo Selo and in Muharine, some 600 m to the southeast, are located in the region of Semberija on the southern fringe of the Carpathian Basin, between the Sava and Drina rivers. Towards the south and west, the plains of Semberija border with the first foothills of Majevica Mountain, which is already on the edge of the Dinaric Alps. Satellite images show the presence of numerous meandering channels in the area, originating from the hydrological activity of the Drina River long before the first human presence in the area. The river activity created a slightly undulating terrain with a gravel base.

Praistorijske grobne humke (tumuli) u sjeveroistočnoj Bosni

Velike humke na lokalitetima Novo Selo i Muharine u ravničarskom predjelu sjeveroistočne Bosne nisu dosada bile zabilježene u arheološkoj literaturi, iako se nalaze na istaknutoj poziciji u neposrednoj blizini grada Bijeljine (Republika Srpska). Prije početka zajedničkog istraživanja u saradnji Instituta OREA i Muzeja Semberije u Bijeljini, starost i funkcija nasutih zemljanih konstrukcija bili su nepoznati. Kako slične humke u bližoj okolini nisu istražene a nisu se mogli konstatovati ni površinski nalazi, karakter ovih impresivnih spomenika napravljenih ljudskom rukom ostao je nedokučiv. Pored toga, intenzivne poljoprivredne aktivnosti u novije vrijeme su dovele do zaravnjavanja i razvlačenja humki, čija je očuvana visina pri početku istraživanja iznosila 1,5 metar.

Pozicija

Istražene i prospekcijskom metodom snimljene humke u Novom Selu kao i humka u Muharinama na oko 600 metara prema jugoistoku, nalaze se u Semberiji na istočnom rubu grada Bijeljine. Ova specifična ravničarska regija između rijeka Save i Drine u širem geografskom okviru predstavlja južni rub Panonske nizije a sa juga i zapada omeđena je prvim obroncima Majevice koja već pripada vjencu Dinarskih planina. Satelitski snimci područja oko Bijeljine na kojem se nalaze pomenute humke jasno pokazuju veliki broj starih riječnih rukavaca nastalih meandriranjem i hidrološkim aktivnostima Drine u vremenu prije prvog ljudskog naseljavanja. Djelovanjem rijeke i riječnih nanosa na ovom dijelu Semberije nastala je blago valovita površina sa riječnim šljunkom kao podlogom.

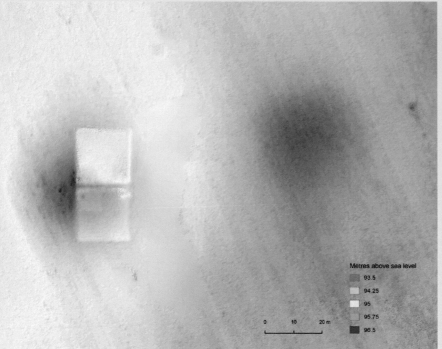

Metres above sea level
93.5
94.25
95
95.75
96.5

0   10   20 m

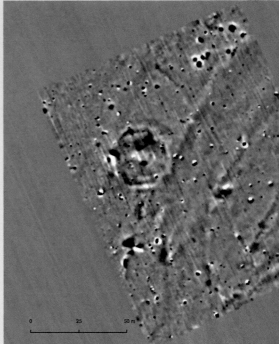

0   25   50 m

Prospections

Geophysical prospection included a wider area around the still easily recognizable elevations in Muharine and Novo Selo. In both cases, the results indicated the existence of circular ditches around the mounds and a number of structures pointing to intensive human activity within the enclosed space. Although the data from the geophysical prospection suggested a structure indicative of large prehistoric burial mounds, it was still unclear from which historical or prehistorical period the construction of the earth mounds originates.

Excavation and Results

In order to verify the results of the geophysical prospection and to determine the age, structure and character of the mounds, excavations were first conducted in Novo Selo. Due to the enormous size, the first step included only the eastern half of the mound. Nevertheless, the amount of soil moved from the surface layers with the help of excavating machines was around 250 tonnes from an area of 800 m^2. The first finds encountered

Prospekcije

Geofizičke prospekcije uključile su šire područje oko još uvijek u lokalnom krajoliku dobro prepoznatljivih humki na lokalitetima Muharine i Novo Selo. U oba slučaja rezultati prospekcije ukazali su na postojanje kružnih jaraka ili rovova u veličini humke, a u unutrašnjem prostoru ustanovljeno je mnoštvo struktura koje svjedoče o intenzivnim ljudskim aktivnostima. Iako su podaci dobiveni geofizičkim snimanjem terena sugerisali raspored kakav je poznat iz praistorijskih grobnih tumula, i dalje nije bilo poznato iz kojeg istorijskog ili praistorijskog perioda potječe gradnja zemljanih humki.

Iskopavanje i rezultati

Sa ciljem da se provjere rezultati geofizičke prospekcije i da se odredi tačna starost, struktura i funkcija zemljanih humki, iskopavanja su prvo pokrenuta na nalazištu Novo Selo. Usljed enormne veličine, prvi korak uključio je istraživanje na istočnoj polovini humke. I pored ovog ograničenja, količina uklonjene zemlje uz pomoć mehanizacije iznosila je oko 250 tona i to samo sa površinskih slojeva na prostiru od oko 800 m². Prve nalaze ispod površinskog sloja predstavljali su skeletni grobovi sa nekoliko komada nakita karakteri-

under the surface layers were two skeletal graves with jewellery typical for the Middle Ages. Further finds followed, which point to a prehistoric use of the mound, including two urn graves and a skeletal grave with the deceased in a crouched position placed on a platform made of river pebbles. Around the pebble platform with the burial, located in a central part of a mound, a reddish layer of burned vegetation was observed. Outside of the burned vegetation layer or on the fringe of the mound, a shallow ditch enclosure that corresponds with the structure captured in the geophysical surveys was also easily recognizable. Finds discovered along the 2 m-wide ditch in irregular deposition pits included broken pottery and animal bones. It was soon clear that the skeletal grave on the pebble platform and the enclosure ditch with animal bones and pottery in an irregular arrangement do not belong to the same period. As the excavation reached the gravel bedrock, it became apparent that the mound was actually built on a natural elevation created by older river activity. In the last step, on the outskirts of the mound a third medieval grave was discovered.

Analyses and Interpretation

The variety of different finds in the eastern half of the mound in Novo Selo revealed the complex and multiphased structure of the burial and ritual place. As the radiocarbon dates confirmed, first activities in Novo Selo took place during the Copper Age (around 3000 BC) with the building of the approximately round enclosure on a natu-

stičnog za srednji vijek. Nakon toga usljedili su nalazi i strukture koji su jasno ukazivali na praistorijski period, uključujući i dvije urne sa kremiranim ljudskim ostacima kao i jedan skeletni grob u zgrčenom položaju koji je bio položen na jednu vrstu platforme napravljane od riječnih oblutaka. Oko platforme sa zgrčenim skeletom, koja se nalazila u centralnom dijelu humke, primjećen je crvenkati sloj sa dobro vidljivim tragovima spaljene vegetacije. Izvan ovog spaljenog sloja odnosno na rubnom dijelu humke, otkriven je i plitki rov koji je po obliku i dimenzijama odgovarao strukturi snimljenoj prilikom geofizičke prospekcije. Duž dva metra širokog rova zabilježeno je nekoliko jama nepravilnog oblika u kojima su se nalazili fragmenti slomljenih keramičkih posuda i životinjske kosti. Na osnovu rasporeda i otkopanih slojeva već u ovoj fazi istraživanja moglo se zaključiti da grob sa zgrčenim pokojnikom na kamenoj platformi i rov sa nepravilnim strukturama ispunjenim keramikom i kostima, ne pripadaju istom periodu. Dostizanjem prirodne podloge od riječnog šljunka također je postalo jasno kako se humka u Novom Selu nalazila na prirodnom uzvišenju nastalom taloženjem riječnih nanosa. Konačno, na rubu humke pronađen je još jedan srednjovjekovni grob.

rally elevated terrain. The animal bones and broken pottery from the same period presumably represent the remains of rituals held within the enclosed space. The two cremation burials in urns also date to the time around 3000 BC and are a further indication that the elevated enclosed space had a ritual character. Striking is also the fact that two urns contained cremated remains of two very old females (60–75 years). It can thus be assumed that during the Copper Age, the natural enclosed elevation in Novo Selo served as a special ritual and burial place for distinct individuals within the society.

More than 1000 years later, in the time between 1800 and 1700 BC, the Bronze Age communities used the elevated terrain for the construction of a burial mound. The central part of the natural elevation was first burned, which could be interpreted as a ritual act. Most of the older, Copper Age structure was probably destroyed during this action. Shortly after burning, an approximately rectangular platform was built directly on the burned vegetation layer by using river pebbles, with bigger pieces on the outside of the construction

Analize i interpretacija

Veliki broj različitih nalaza i struktura na istočnoj polovini humke u Novom Selu ukazao je na kompleksnu strukturu i višefaznu upotrebu ovog grobnog odnosno ritualnog mjesta. Rezultati radiokarbonskih analiza potvrdili su da prve aktivnosti datiraju u bakarno doba (oko 3000 p. n. e.) kada je na blago povišenom prirodnom terenu napravljen približno kružni rov. Nalazi keramike i životinjskih kostiju iz istog perioda vjerovatno predstavljaju ostatke ritualnih radnji unutar ograđenog prostora. Dva groba u urnama potječu također iz ovog vremena i dodatna su indikacija kako je ograđeni prostor na prirodnoj uzvisini bio ritualnog karaktera. Upadljiva je također činjenica kako spaljeni ostaci u obje urne pripadaju ženskim osobama visoke starosti (60–75 godina). Prema tome, može se pretpostaviti kako je prirodna uzvisina u za vrijeme bakarnog doba predstavljala ograđeno ritualno i grobno mjesto na kojem su očigledno sahranjivani samo određeni članovi zajednice.

Preko 1000 godina kasnije, u vrijeme između 1800 i 1700 p. n. e. zajednice bronzanog doba iskoristile su povišeni teren za podizanje grobne humke. Centralni dio uzvišenja prvo je spaljen, što bi se također moglo interpretirati kao ritualni čin. Većina starijih strukura iz bakarnog doba je ovim radnjama vjerovatno uništena. Neposredno nakon paljenja na izgorenom vegetacijskom sloju sagrađena je platforma od naslaganih riječnih oblutaka, pri čemu su veći komadi postavljani sa vanjske strane a manji komadi oko dijela na kojem je bio položen pokojnik. Kod sahranjene osobe se radilo o muškarcu u dobi između 21 i 25 godina. Pravilni četverougaoni obrisi oko zgrčenog skeleta ukazivali su

and smaller stones around the place for the deceased. The buried person was determined as a young male (21–25 years). The clear rectangular shapes around the crouched skeleton pointed at additional construction elements. The remains of wooden planks confirmed the assumption that the buried individual was laying on a four-grip wooden stretcher or a comparable barrow that was put on top of the stone platform, probably in the course of the burial ceremony. Moreover, rows of smaller postholes around the pebble platform evidenced that the grave was inside an object or within the fence, which probably had the function of a mortuary. Subsequently, the burial ground was covered with layers of soil that created a mound or a burial tumulus.

Although the young male was buried without any grave goods or prestigious objects, the huge effort made by the community to build the burial place and to heap up an enormous amount of soil speaks for a prominent role within the Bronze Age community of this area.

In the Middle Ages, the elevation of the mound was also used as a burial place. Three identified skeletal graves were badly preserved due to the shallow position and the impact of fertilizer. Nevertheless, a characteristic bronze earring and an iron belt buckle can clearly be associated with the attire of the period between the 11th and the 13th century AD. It is important to stress that these are the first burials from this period in the region of Semberija.

Finally, the radiocarbon results of a few burned features within the tumulus as well as a few finds of pottery speak for a temporal use of the mound in Novo Selo during the Ottoman period or between the 16th and 17th centuries AD. The purpose of the latest occupation remains unknown since no graves or other characteristic objects could be identified.

Summary and Outlook

The investigations of the newly discovered burial ground in Novo Selo provided the first insights into the complex burial rituals of Copper Age and Bronze Age communities in the border region of Semberija between the Carpathian Basin and the Balkans. The slightly elevated and easily seen spots in the local plain landscape were obviously used as burial and ritual grounds and as a starting point for the construction of mounds. The proximity of a second mound in Muharine with comparable results in the geophysical survey leads to the conclusion that burial tumuli had a decisive role in the creation of a ritual and cultural prehistoric landscape. The research commenced within the framework of the project "Visualizing the unknown Balkans" offers a good starting point for future archaeological activities that will certainly contribute toward a better understanding and interpretation of the local and regional landscape.

na postojanje još nekih dodatnih elemenata u sklopu grobne konstrukcije. Pronađeni ostaci dasaka potvrdili su pretpostavku da je preminula osoba ležala na jednoj vrsti drvenog nosila ili na nekoj sličnoj konstrukciji sa četiri jasno prepoznatljiva produženja odnosno rukohvata. U sklopu ceremonije ukopa, drvena nosila sa pokojnikom položena su na vrh kamene platforme. Pored toga, oko kamene platforme otkriveni su pravilni redovi manjih rupa za stubove ili kolčiće koji su svjedočili kako se grob zapravo nalazio unutar nekog manjeg objekta ili unutar ograde. Funkcija ovog objekta ili ograde bila je da se dodatno istakne odnosno označi ukopno mjesto u smislu posebnog objekta za preminulog. Poslije toga, grob i njegova neposredna okolina su zatrpani slojem zemlje koji je na kraju i doveo do stvaranja uzvišenja odnosno do konačnog izgleda tumula.

Iako u grobu muškraca sahranjenog u zgrčenom položaju nisu pronađeni nikakvi grobni prilozi ili prestižni predmeti, ogromna količina uloženog rada pri gradnji grobnog mjesta te posebno pri nasipanju zemljane humke govore u prilog pretpostavci kako se ipak radilo o istaknutom odnosno posebnom članu bronzanodobne zajednice u ovoj regiji.

U srednjem vijeku humka je ponovo korištena kao grobno mjesto. Tri pronađena skeletna groba bila su izraziro loše očuvana zbog male dubine i zbog djelovanje umjetnog gnjojiva sa poljoprivrednog zemljišta. Ipak, pronađena bronzana naušnica i gvozdeni dio opasača mogu se nesumnjivo pripisati periodu između 11. i 13. vijeka n.e. Potrebno je istaknuti kako je riječ je prvim grobovima iz ovoga vremena na prostoru Semberije.

Konačno, rezultati radiokarbonskih analiza na uzrocima iz nekoliko jako izgorenih struktura kao i pojedinačni nalazi keramike upućuju kako je tumul u Novom Selu korišten i za vrijeme osmanskog perioda odnosno u toku 16. i 17. vijeka n. e. Kako nisu pronađeni niti grobovi niti neki drugi objekti iz ovog vremena, ostaje nepoznato kakvu je tumul imao namjenu u ovom periodu.

Zaključak i perspektive

Istraživanja na novootkrivenom grobnom mjestu na lokalitetu Novo Selo pružila su prvi uvid u kompleksne pogrebne rituale zajednica bakarnog i bronzanog doba u Semberiji kao graničnoj regiji između Panonske nizije i Balkana. Blago uzvišena i samim tim lako vidljiva mjesta u lokanom ravničarskom krajoliku očigledno su korištena kao ritualna i grobna mjesta te kao početna tačka za gradnju impozantnih zemljanih humki. Blizi- na druge humke u Muharinama na kojoj su rezultati geofizičke prospekcije ukazali na postojanje sličnih struktura kao i u Novom Selu, navodi na zaključak kako su tumuli sa ukopanim, istaknutim članovima zajednice imali ključnu ulogu u stvaranju ritualnog i kulturnog krajolika u praistoriji ovog podneblja. Započeta istraživanja u sklopu projekta „Vizualizacija nepoznatog Balkana" predstavljaju dobru osnovu za nastavak arheoloških iskopavanja koja bi svakako pridonijela boljoj i potpunijoj rekonstrukciji i interpretaciji u lokalnim i regionalnim okvirima.

BRONZE AGE METALLURGY IN EAST SERBIA

BRONZANODOBNA METALURGIJA U ISTOČNOJ SRBIJI

Mario Gavranović / Aleksandar Kapuran / Mathias Mehofer / Lukas Waltenberger

Rudna Glava ⚒

Trnjane
Hajdučka Česma ● ● Ružana
Čoka Njica

Sava

Great Morava

West Morava South Morava

Danube

Vardar

Drina

Drava

0   50
━━━━━
km

Bronze Age Metallurgy in East Serbia

The copper ore deposits in eastern Serbia between the cities Majdenpek and Bor are among the largest in Europe with a long exploitation history starting with the earliest Copper Age (c. 5000–4500 BC) and lasting until the present time. The famous site Rudna Glava represents one of the earliest copper ore mines, discovered and used by the communities of the Vinča culture during the Neolithic. The importance and crucial role of the site Rudna Glava for the development of metallurgy in our continent is widely acknowledged among both archaeometallurgists and prehistorians.

However, in contrast to the large number of studies dedicated to Copper Age metallurgy in eastern Serbia, our knowledge about Bronze Age developments in this region is still extremely limited. During this period (between 2300

Bronzanodobna metalurgija u istočnoj Srbiji

Ležista bakarne rude u istočnoj Srbiji između gradova Majdanpeka i Bora ubrajaju se među najveća u Evropi a njihova eksploatacija započela je već u bakarnom dobu (5000–4500 p. n. e.) i traje do današnjih vremena. Poznato nalazišta Rudna glava jedan je od najstarijih rudnika bakra kojeg su otkrili i koristili pripadnici Vinčanske kulture tokom neolita. Važnost i posebna uloga nalazišta Rudna glava u razvoju metalurgije na našem kontinentu već je odavno priznata od strane arheometalurga i arheologa praistoričara.

Za razliku od mnogobrojnih studija posvećenih najranijoj metalurgiji bakaranog doba, razvoj ove aktivnosti na području istočne Srbije tokom bronzanog doba je još uvek većim delom nepoznat. Za vreme ovog perioda odnosno između 2300 i 1000 p. n. e., dobijeni bakar služio je kao osnovna sirovina za leguru sa kalajem i dobivanje novog metala koji je dao ime celoj praistorijskoj epohi – bronzano doba.

Prvi čvrsti dokazi o postojanju metalurških aktivnosti na teritoriji istočne Srbije u vreme bronzanog doba otkriveni su u ranijim iskopavanjima nalazišta Trnjane (1985–1998) i Ružana (2013–2015). Brojni nalazi metalične šljake, kao otpadnog proizvoda prilikom topljenja bakarne rude, potvrdili su da su zajednice bronzanog doba prerađivale bakarnu rudu i proizvodile dragocenu sirovinu. Istraživanja u nalazištu Trnjane dovela su i do otkrića nekropole sa urnama u neposrednoj blizini naselja koja je omogućila da se dobije prvi uvid u do tada jedinstvene pogrebne običaje lokalnih zajednica na teritoriji Srbije. Urne sa kremiranim ostacima pokojinka postavljane su unutar kružno naslaganih kamenih konstrukcija promera između 2 i 4 metra. Činjenica da u grobovima na Trnjanima uglavnom nisu pronađeni specifični grobni prilozi (delovi nošnje ili oružje) otežavala je preciznu dataciju ovog groblja. Većim delom nepoznat ostao je i tehnološki kontekst metalurških aktivnosti, socijalna struktura zajednica uključenih u proizvodnju metala kao i njihova uloga u široj mreži razmena bronzanodobne Evrope.

Prospekcije i istraživanja 2017–2019

U sklopu novog istraživačkog projekta austrijskih i srpskih stručnjaka koji je započeo 2017 godine obavljene su intenzivne prospekcije a zatim i arheološka iskopavanja na lokalitetima Trnjane, Hajdučka česma i Čoka Njica, koji se svi nalaze u blizini grada Bora. Za razliku od nalazišta Trnjane na kojem su i ranije vršena arheološka istraživanja, tragovi bronzanodobne aktivnosti na nalazištima Hajdučka česma i Čoka Njica bili su poznati samo kroz površinske nalaze ili slučajne predmete pronađene prilikom građevinskih radova.

Prvi korak u sklopu prospekcija činila su nedestruktivna geofizička snimanja terena sa ciljem da se identfikuju tragovi praistorijskih struktura (grobovi, jame, podnice kuća kao i mesta prerade bakarne rude). Posle toga, na šumovitom području na kojem se nalaze spomenuti lokaliteti izvršeno je lasersko snimanje iz vazduha tehnikom LiDAR čime se dobio digitalni visinski model zemljišta. Ovaj metod primjenjen je kako bi se otkrili svi ljudskom rukom prouzrokovani zahvati koji bi se mogli povezati za aktivnostima za vreme bronzanog doba (okna, šljakišta, odbrambeni jarci).

Intenzivne prospekcije jasno su pokazale da naselja iz bronzanog doba kao što su Trnjane ili Čoka Njica nisu bila utvrđena pošto se na snimcima nisu primetili nikave tragovi odbrambenih odnosno fortifikacijskih elemenata (bedemi, jarci, rovovi). Geofizička snimanja potvrdila su međutim postojanje mnogobrojnih struktura unutar ispitanih nalazišta te tako i odredila tok predstojećih iskopavanja.

and 1000 BC), the extracted copper served as a raw material for an alloy with tin and creation of a new metal that gave the name for a whole epoch – the Bronze Age.

The earlier excavations in the sites Trnjane (1985–1998) and Ružana (2013–2015) near the city of Bor provided first tangible evidence about metallurgical activity in eastern Serbia during the Bronze Age. The numerous pieces of metallic slag, a waste product of copper ore smelting, confirmed that the Bronze Age societies were also involved in metal extraction and production of the desired raw material. Moreover, the investigations in Trnjane also led to the discovery of an urn cemetery in the immediate vicinity of the settlement that offered a first insight into the distinctive burial practices of local communities. The urns with the cremated human remains were placed in circular stone constructions with a diameter of between 2 and 4 metres. However, the fact that graves in Trnjane contained no specific objects (personal attire, weapons) made it difficult to estimate the precise dating of the cemetery. Still less known was the technological context of the metallurgical activities, the social background of metal-producing communities and their role in the overall exchange network of Bronze Age Europe.

Prospections and Investigations 2017–2019

The new Austrian-Serbian project started in 2017 included intensive prospection and subsequent excavations at the sites Trnjane, Hajdučka Česma and Čoka Njica, all situated near the city of Bor. While Trnjane had already been archaeologically investigated, Hajdučka Česma and Čoka Njica were recognized as Bronze Age sites only by surface finds and chance discoveries in the course of construction work.

The first step of the prospections involved non-destructive geophysical surveys with the aim of identifying traces of prehistoric structures (graves, pits, house floors, and copper ore smelting places). After that, airborne laser scanning (LiDAR) was carried out in a forested area of the sites covering 10 km² and creating the digital elevation model of the area. This method was used in order to detect all intrusions that could be connected with the Bronze Age activities in the area (e.g. mining shafts, slag dumps, ditches).

The extensive prospection revealed that the Bronze Age settlements Trnjane or Čoka Njica, were not fortified since no ramparts or any other fortifications could be observed on the elevation model. Geophysical surveys indicated a number of potential prehistoric structures and set the course for the upcoming excavations.

Trnjane

The new excavations in a settlement area of Trnjane yielded a great number of finds, including pottery, stone tools, animal bones and metallic slag. The Bronze Age settlement spread over several terraces flanked by higher hills and thus created the setting of a natural amphitheatre. The urn cemetery with 43 discovered graves was located just to the east of a settlement area. According to the results of anthropological analyses of cremated human remains, all age groups are represented in the cemetery, including newborns and a pregnant female. The rare grave

N

0   2,5   5 m

Trnjane

Nova iskopavanja na lokalitetu Trnjane dovela su do otkrića velikog broja nalaza uključujući keramiku, kamene alatke, životinjske kosti i metaličnu šljaku. Naselje iz bronzanog doba prostiralo se na nekoliko susednih terasa koje su sa strana oivičene uzvišenjima. Groblje sa urnama sa ukupno 43 otkrivena groba nalazilo se neposredno uz istočni rub naselja. Sudeći prema rezultatima antropološke analize kremiranih ostataka, među spaljenim pokojnicima su zastupljene sve dobne kategorije, uključujući i novorođenčad i trudnice. Retki grobni nalazi sastojali su se od jednog bronzanog noža, kamene sekire, keramičke lampe, vretena i manjih posuda (pehari i šoljice).

Zahvaljujući novim istraživanjima, po prvi put se stvorila mogućnost za rekonstrukciju metalurških procesa topljenja bakarne rude koji su se odvijali u krugu naselja. Razni oblici metalične šljake upućuju na najmanje tri različita stepena to-

goods included a bronze knife, a stone axe and a ceramic lamp, spindle whorls and smaller vessels (beakers and cups). It is further interesting that the size of the circular stone grave monuments does not correlate with the age of the deceased.

Thanks to the new investigation, it was also possible for the first time to reconstruct the metallurgical processes of ore smelting which took place within the settlement area. The various shapes of metallic slag point to at least three different steps in copper ore smelting with raw copper metal as a final product. The Bronze Age community in Trnjane was primarily engaged in the separation of copper from local ores since traces of the alloying of copper and tin or bronze production are completely lacking.

The recent excavations in Trrnjane also provided a sufficient number of organic samples (animal bones, burned seeds) for more precise dating of the Bronze Age occupation with the help of the radiocarbon method. At the same time, it was also possible to apply the same dating method to the cremation remains from urns. The results from both settlement and cemetery clearly show that Trnjane was occupied between the 19th and the 17th centuries BC, which is significantly older than the previously assumed age (c. 14th–11th centuries BC).

Čoka Njica and Ružana

The sites Ružana and Čoka Njica are located 1 km and 3.5 km to the southeast of Trnjane on the same slope above the small river Brestovačka reka. The earlier small-scale excavations in Ružana brought to light a significant amount of metallic slag and the remains of smelting installations, found together with characteristic Bronze Age pottery of a type also found in nearby Trnjane. The detailed analyses of slags in terms of their chemical composition revealed that Ružana and Trnjane both used the same ores and applied a very similar technique for copper extraction. The clear evidence that two nearby smelting places existed during the same period came with the radiocarbon dates from Ružana that indicate the same period (19th–17th centuries BC) as for Trnjane.

Another copper production settlement from the same period is Čoka Njica, situated on a high, spacious plateau overlooking the local landscape around the city of Bor. Until the start of the project, the site was known only by chance finds of pottery and metallic slag from the surface. The extensive geophysical prospection on the plateau identified a variety of potential structures that could not be clearly assessed without excavations. The subsequent field actions confirmed the postulation that Čoka Njica is also a Bronze Age site involved in copper production. A remarkable smelting installation made of clay and stones was uncovered in one of the trenches, together with

pljenja rude sa čistim bakrom kao završnim proizvodima. Bronzanodobna zajednica na lokalitetu Trnjane primarno je bila uključena u proces izdvajanja bakra iz ruda, dok tragovi dalje prerade bakra odnosno legiranja bakra sa kalajem i dobivanja bronze za sada u potpunosti nedostaju.

Novijim iskopavanjima unutar naselja dobiven je i dovoljan broj organskih nalaza (životinjske kosti, izgorena semena biljaka) kojima je, uz pomoć radiokarbonske metode, bilo moguće preciznije odrediti starost naseljavanja u toku bronzanog doba. U isto vreme, ovaj metod primenjen je i na uzorcima kremiranih pokojnika iz urni na nekropoli. Rezultati ovih analiza jasno su ukazali kako naselje i nekropola na lokalitetu Trnjane pripadaju periodu između 19. i 17. veka p.n.e., što je znatno starije nego što se predpostavljalo u ranijim istraživanjima (između 14. i 11. veka p. n. e.)

Čoka Njica i Ružana

Lokaliteti Ružana i Čoka Njica smešteni su 1 km odnosno 3,5 kilometra jugoistočno od Trnjana na padininma istog uzvišenju koje se pruža iznad Brestovačke reke. Ranijim iskopavanjima na Ružani je otkrivena veća količina metalične šljake kao i ostaci peći za topljenje bakarne rude, koji su pronađni zajedno za bronzanodobnom keramikom istog tipa kao i na nalazištu Trnjane. Detaljene hemijske analize sastava šljake pokazale su da je i na Ružani i na Trnjanima prerađivana ista bakarna ruda koristeći vrlo sličnu tehnologiju izdvajanja metala. Konačan dokaz da su oba mesta postojala kroz isto vreme pružili su radiokarbonski datum sa Ružane koji upućuju na isti period (19.–17. vek p.n.e) kao i datumi sa neznatno udaljenih Trnjana.

Lokalitet Čoka Njica predstavlja još jedno nalazište sa tragovima prerade bakarne rude. Čoka Njica je smeštena na visokom, prostranom platou sa kojeg se dobro vidi cela okolina grada Bora i dolina Brestovačke reke. Pre početka istraživanja, ovo nalazište je bilo poznato po površinskim nalazima keramike i šljaka. Geofizičke prospekcije na celom prostoru platoa naznačile su postojanje raznovrsnih struktura i potencijalnih objekata čija se starost i funkcija nije mogla jasno proceniti bez dodatnih iskopavanja. Arheološkim istraživanjima koja su usledila potvrdilo se kako se i kod Čoka Njice radi o lokalitetu iz bronzanog doba na kojem se prerađivala bakarna ruda i proizvodio bakar. U jednoj od istraživanih sondi pronađeni su ostaci topioničke peći napravljene od kamena i gline, zajedno sa mnoštvom keramičkih sudova, metalične šljake i nekoliko kapljica čistog bakra kao finalnog proizvoda. Radiokarbonski datumi dobiveni iz uzoraka životinjskih kostiju i ostataka izgorenog drveta potvrdili su da metalurška aktivnost na lokalitetu Čoka Njica također datira u vreme između 18. i 17 veka p. n. e. Prve hemijske analize komada metalične šljake upućuju da je peć otkrivena na Čoka Njici najverovatnije služila za rafinaciju bakra u zadnjem koraku dobijanja metala iz rude.

metallic slags, a massive quantity of pottery vessels and a few drops of pure copper. The animal bones and remains of burned wood provided samples for radiocarbon dating, which corroborated the assumption that the metallurgical activity in Čoka Njica also took place in the 18th and 17th centuries BC. Judging by the first analyses of the metallic slag, the installation in Čoka Njica was used to refine copper in the last step of extraction processes.

Hajdučka Česma

Hajdučka Česma is situated in the valley of Brestovačka reka, just about 1.5 km to the southwest of Trnjane. The first urns came to light in the 1990s during construction work. However, it was only the geophysical prospection in 2017 that indicated the size and extent of a cemetery that spread over several gently sloping terraces with far more than the assumed 100 burials in similar grave constructions to those in Trnjane. The subsequent excavations led to the discovery of 14 urn graves with well-preserved stone constructions just under the modern surface. In some of the graves additional smaller vessels were also found on the fringe of the stone monuments, indicating ritual activities (feasting) in the course of the burial ceremony. A few urns also had a bowl on the top that served as a lid. The repertoire of grave goods, which were found both inside and outside the urns, included spindle whorls, small ceramic lamps, one bronze sewing needle and a variety of small jugs and cups.

The analyses of cremated human remains pointed at a very high burning temperature (800°C and more) and the presence of all body parts, with an occasional anatomic layering within the urn, meaning that lower parts of the body were put in the bottom of the urn, while the fragments of the scull came on the top. Regarding the age of the deceased, children and young adults clearly prevail, while the older individu-   als are missing thus far. One of the urns contained the remains of a young female and a newborn.

The radiocarbon dates from all excavated graves imply use of the burial place in the time between the 20th and the 18th centuries BC, which means that the burial place in Hajdučka Česma is slightly older than the graves in nearby Trnjane, although for the most part both burial places existed during the same time. The associated settlement of the cemetery in Hajdučka Česma has, however, still not been identified and that remains one of the important tasks for the future.

Hajdučka česma

Hajdučka česma smeštena je u dolini Brestovačke reke, samo oko 1,5 km vazdušnom linijom jugozapadno od Trnjana. Prve urne odnosno prvi grobovi pronađeni su u 1990-im godinama prilikom građevinskih radova. Međutim tek su geofizičke prospekcije iz 2017 godine ukazale na veličinu i rasprostiranje nekropole koja se pruža preko nekoliko blagih terasa i obuhvata oko 100 grobnih konstrukcija sličnog tipa kao i na nekropoli Trnjane. U iskopavanjima koja su započeta nakon prospekcije, otkriveno je 14 grobova u urnama sa dobro očuvanim kružnim kamenim konstrukcijama koje su se nalazile neposredno ispod današnje površine. U nekim grobovima zabeležene su i manje posude na rubovima kamenih konstrukcija, koje upućuju na ritualne ili ceremonijalne radnje za vreme i posle ukopa. Neke od urni bile su također pokrivene zdelama koje su služile kao poklopci. Repertoar grobnih priloga koji su otkriveni u urnama zajedno sa kremiranim ljudskim ostacima ali i pored urni, uključuje keramička vretena, male keramičke lampe, jednu bronzanu iglu za šivanje kao i raznovrsne manje vrčeve, pehare i šolje.

Analiza kremiranih ljudskih ostataka pokazala je kako su pokojnici spaljivani na vrlo visokim temperaturama (800°C i više) a u urnama su bili prisutni svi delovi tela uz povremeni anatomski raspored kostiju, što znači da su donji delovi tela stavljani na dno urne, dok su ostaci lobanje polagani na vrh. U pogledu starosti spaljenih pokojnika, preovladavaju deca i adolescenti a urne sa ostacima starijih osoba za sada nisu pronađene. U jednoj od urni ustanovljeni su ostaci mlađe osobe ženskog spola i novorođenčeta.

Radiokarbonski datumi koji su urađeni za sve otkrivene grobove upućuju da se grobno mesto koristilo između 20. i 18. veka p. n. e. što bi značilo kako su neki grobovi neznatno stariji nego na Trnjanima ali obe nekropole najvećim su delom postojale kroz isti vremenski period. Pripadajuće naselje nekropole na Hajdučkoj česmi još uvek nije otkriveno i to je jedan od glavnih zadataka u budućim istraživanjima.

Summary and Outlook

The joint research by Austrian and Serbian experts on eastern Serbia in the region over the past three years significantly expanded our knowledge about the Bronze Age societies in this part of the Balkans. Intensive prospection and field activities resulted in the detection of new archaeological sites engaged in copper production and associated cemeteries with urn cremation graves. Thanks to the series of radiocarbon dates, it is finally possible to pinpoint the age of new and old sites. The anthropological analyses provided further information about the individuals buried in the urns within the round stone monuments. The involvement of metallurgical experts helped greatly in understanding the process of metal extraction from the local copper ore. The general lack of bronze objects in the investigated sites implies that the copper produced there was traded to other regions. One of the focal questions is which regions or workshops were the main customers for the copper from eastern Serbia? The achievements of the project "Vizualizing the unknown Balkans" provided an excellent starting point for the new, follow-up research project "New insights in Bronze Age metal producing societies" (2019–2022) supported by the Austrian Science Fund (FWF).

Zaključak i perspektiva istraživavanja

Zajednička naučna istraživanja austrijskih i srpskih stručnjaka u zadnje tri godina u istočnoj Srbiji značajno su pridonela boljem poznavanju zajednica bronzanog doba u ovom delu Balkana. Intenzivne prospekcije i naknadna iskopavanja dovela su otkrića novih arheoloških nalazišta na kojima je konstatovana prerada i topljenje bakarne rude kao i do otkrića vezanih uz pripadajuće nekropole sa urnama. Zahvaljuući radiokarbonskim datumima moguće je izneti preciznije podatke o datovanju istraženih lokaliteta. Antropološke analize kremiranih ostataka iz urni pružile su pri tome niz novih podataka o spaljenim pokojnicima. Uključivanje stručnjaka za metalurgiju umnogome je doprinelo razjašnjavanju procesa koji vode od prerade i topljenja rude do dobivanja čistog bakra. Opšti nedostatak bronzanih predmeta u celoj regiji navodi na zaključak da je dobiveni bakar verovatno prosleđivan odnosno razmenjivan u druge regije. Jedno od centralnih pitanja budućih istraživanja je gde je završavao bakar iz istočne Srbije odnosno koje regionalne radionice su koristile tu sirovinu. Rezultati projekta "Vizualizacija nepoznatog Balkana" u ovoj specifičnoj regiji pružila su osnovu za pokretanje novog zajedničkog istraživačkog projekta pod nazivom "New insights in Bronze Age metal producing societies" (2019–2022) koji je podržao Austrijski naučni fond (FWF).

BRONZE AGE COMMUNITIES IN CENTRAL BOSNIA

BRONČANO DOBA U SREDNJOJ BOSNI

Mario Gavranović / Irene M. Petschko

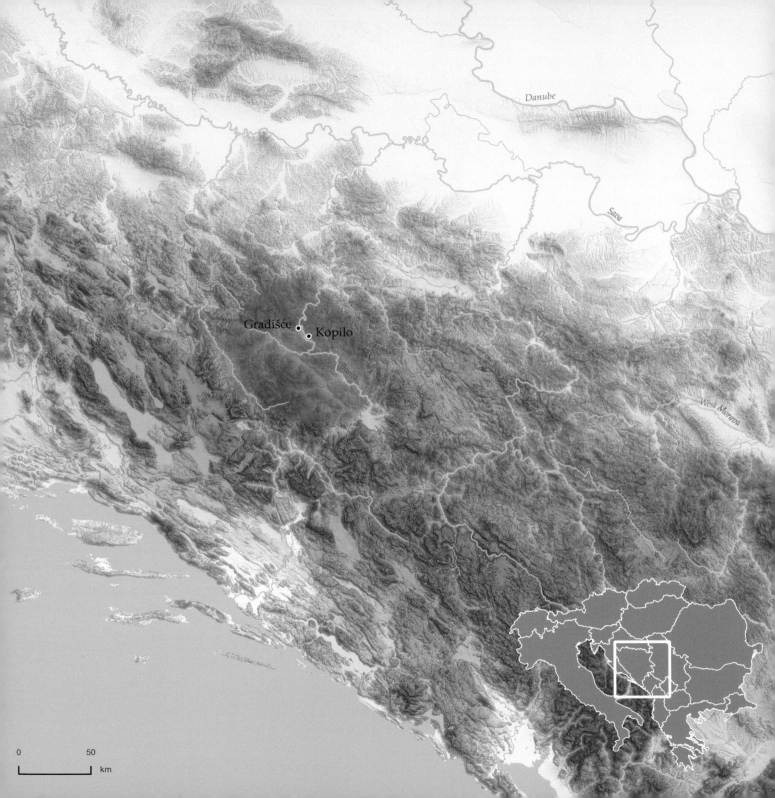

Gradišće • • Kopilo

Danube

Sava

Drina

West Morava

Bosna

0   50
⊢——————⊣ km

Bronze Age Communities in Central Bosnia

Moving Up

During the Bronze Age, which in this area approximately corresponds with the time of the 2nd millennium BC (2000–1000 BC), people in the Dinaric Alps left the valley plains to settle on plateaus in higher elevations in order to take advantage of the dominant strategic position overlooking river valleys and basins. To research the settlement pattern in the mountain zone during the Bronze and the Iron Age, the Zenica Basin, which is part of the Bosna Valley, was chosen. The Bosna, a tributary of the Sava, is one of the major rivers which connect the Adriatic Sea with the Carpathian Basin, and therefore was and is a vital artery through the ages until modern times. Considering this favourable geostrategic position, it is not surprising that 19 hilltop settlements roughly dating to the Bronze and Iron Ages have been recorded around Zenica so far. Only one has been excavated, so little is known about their individual layout, extent and exact date of settlement activity as well as networks between contemporaneous sites. The goal of the project is to kick off research in this micro-region. To achieve this, the project cooperated with the Zenica City Museum. The first steps of investigations included intensive geophysical prospection of several sites, followed shortly afterwards by airborne laser scanning of an area of c. 12 ha.

Revealing Prehistory

Two hill chains – Kopilo and Gradišće – constitute promising research spots due to their prominent location. They are located on the opposite sides of the Bosna River, overlooking the entrance and the exit to the Zenica Basin, but are also in direct visual contact with one another. Airborne laser scans (LiDAR) reveal the topography and remains of human historical and prehistorical activity (ramparts, ditches, plateaus, stone mounds), beneath the dense forests. The digital elevation model created as an outcome of airborne laser scans complements the information obtained by surveys and geophysical prospection.

Stone Monuments for the Dead?

The 2019 excavations kicked off by investigating two of the stone tumuli at Gradišće

Brončano doba u srednjoj Bosni

Naseljavanje visinskih položaja

Tokom brončanog doba, koje o ovoj regiji smještenoj unutar Dinarskih planina uglavnom odgovora vremenu drugog milenijuma p. n. e. (2000–1000 p. n. e.), dolazi do intenzivnijeg naseljavanja dominantnih i strateški povoljno smještenih platoa na uzvisinama sa kojih se pruža dobar pregled okolnih riječnih dolina i kotlina.

Istraživanja u Zeničkom bazenu rijeke Bosne pokrenuta su sa ciljem boljeg upoznavanja dinamike brončanodobnog i željeznodobnog naseljavanja. Rijeka Bosna jedna je od najvećih pritoka Save te već od prahistorijskih vremena predstavlja iznimno važnu komunikaciju između Jadrana i Panonske nizije čiji se značaj nije izgubio ni do današnjih dana.

Uzimajući u obzir povoljan geostrateški položaj, činjenica da je na ovom području dosada registrirano 19 visinskih naselja iz brončanog ili željeznog doba nije iznenađujuća. Međutim do sada je samo jedno naselje djelomično arheološki istraženo tako da su saznanja o obliku, veličini, preciznijem datiranju kao i međusobnoj vezi između istovremenih naselja ostala dosta skromna. Zato je jedan od primarnih zadataka pokrenutog projekta bio da se intenziviraju istraživanja u specifičnoj mikroregiji Zeničkog bazena. Prvi korak predstavljalo je uspostavljanje institucionalne suradnje sa Muzejem grada Zenice nakon čega su uslijedile intenzivne geofizičke prospekcije na nekoliko lokaliteta a zatim i snimanje iz zraka tehnikom LiDAR na području od oko 12 ha.

Otkrivanje prahistorije

Niz lokaliteta na sedlastom grebenu iznad mjesta Gradišće kao i nalazište Kopilo izdvajaju se među ostalim visinskim naseljima usljed svoje istaknute pozicije. Gradišće i Kopilo smješteni su na suprotnim stranama rijeke Bosne te kontroliraju ulaznu i izlaznu situaciju u Zenički bazen a pored toga stoje i u međusobnom vizualnom kontaktu. Digitalni visinski model terena dobiven laserskim snimanjem iz zraka otkrio je izgled topografije ispod dijelova pokrivenih gustom šumom te naznačio niz struktura koje se mogu interpretirati kao tragovi ljudskih aktivnosti u historijskom i prahistorijskom periodu (bedemi, rovovi, zaravnati platoi, humke sa naslaganim kamenom). Informacije vidljive na topografskom modelu upotpunjene su zatim rezultatima geofizičkih snimanja kao i intenzivnim rekognosciranjem terena.

Kameni spomenici za mrtve?

Iskopavanja u 2019. godini započela su istraživanjem dvije kamene gomile na grebenu iznad Gradišća sa cilljem da se otkrije njihova struktura i preciznije odredi starost i funkcija. Činjenica da se kamene humke mogu dobro razaznati na digitalnom topografskom modelu omogućila je da se svi potencijalni tumuli na danas šumovitom području provjere na licu mjesta te zatim i kartiraju. Pokazalo se kako se kamene gomile prije svega prostiru duž hrbata grebena koji ujedno služi i kao najbolja komunikacija a uglavnom su se nalazili u manjim grupama.

with the aim of recording their structure, dating their formation and finding hints as to their function. Their visibility on the digital elevation model allowed a systematic survey of all suspected stone mounds and mapping thereof. The stone monuments are distributed along the hill ridge, where moving is easiest, and are encountered in groups.

Clear traces of prehistoric activity were unearthed in a stone mound described as Tumulus 1. After the topsoil and several layers of stones were removed, it was possible to document a circular wall made of large flat stones. Within the enclosed space, several prehistoric pottery sherds were found, which most likely originate from the Bronze Age. These remain the only finds from the centre of Tumulus 1, which was most likely disturbed and then closed again a long time ago. While a date for the construction of the tumulus is not yet known, the stone wall indicates construction with a purpose – probably burial – in mind.

Watching Who is Coming and Going

The Ravna plateau on the eastern end of the hill chain over Gradišće is closest to where the Bosna exits the Zenica Basin and flows toward the north. This strategically remarkable place makes it a prime target for research activities. Excavations were conducted with the goal of investigating the prehistoric settlement, which was only known from stray finds until that point. The digital elevation model suggests that the plateau seems to have been artificially enlarged to increase the available space while it is well protected by the steep hill slopes.

Due to modern agriculture, the uncovered prehistoric contexts were heavily disturbed, so while pottery, chipped stone and animal bones were among the finds, no information on settlement structures is available for now. A C14 sample was taken from an animal bone. It dates to the 12th century BCE and therefore proves the presence of humans on Ravna during the later stages of the Bronze Age.

*

The third site that was excavated during the 2019 season was the hilltop settlement of Kopilo, which overlooks the entrance of the Bosna River into the Zenica Basin. The hill is protected by steep slopes on three sides

Najjasniji tragovi koji upućuju na prahistorijsku aktivnost pronađeni su u kamenoj gomili označenoj kao tumul 1. Nakon što su otklonjeni površinki slojevi te nekoliko naslaga kamenja, zabilježen je kružni zid izgrađen od posloženih kamenih ploča većih dimenzija. Unutar ovoga zida pronađeno je više fragmenata prahistorijske keramike koja se može pripisati brončanom dobu. Kako unutar ove centralne konstrukcije nisu pronađeni nikakvi drugi predmeti, može se pretpostaviti kako je tumul 1 već u vrijeme kratko nakon podizanja otvaran i manipuliran a zatim ponovo zatvoren. Iako ne postoje sigurni podaci o svrsi kamene konstrukcije, naslagani kameni zid ukazuje na određenu namjenu u kontekstu grobne arhitekture.

Pregled ulaza i izlaza

Plato po imenom Ravna nalazi sa na istočnom rubu sedlastog grebena iznad Gradišća. Plato je smješten na uzvišenju direktno iznad mjesta gdje rijeka Bosna napušta Zenički bazen i teče dalje prema sjeveru. Ovaj izniman strateški položaj bio je je jedan od glavnih razloga za pokretanje iskopavanja sa ciljem da se bolje istraže ostaci praistorijskog naselja čije se postojanje moglo pretpostaviti na osnovu površinskih nalaza. Digitalni topografski model platoa upućivao je na dodatna, ciljana proširenja zaravnatog prostora koji je sa svih strana bio dobro zašitićen strmim padinama.

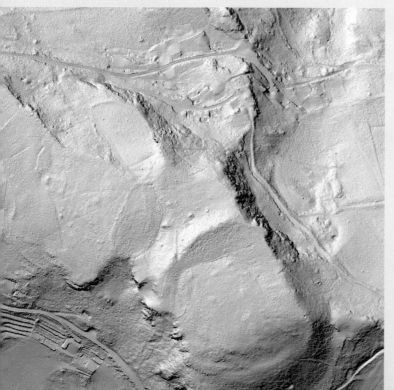

Pokazalo se kako su strukture i slojevi na platou Ravna uglavnom uništene modernim poljoprivrednim radovima, no pronađen je veliki broj fragmenata keramičkih posuda, kamenih alatki i životinjskih kostiju u sekundarnom položaju koji jasno ukazuju na prahistorijsko obitavanje na ovom položaju. O samom izgledu, veličini i rasporedu naselja zasada se ne mogu donijeti nikakve konkretne ocjene. Radiokarbonski datumi iz uzorka pronađenih životnjskih kostiju datiraju u 12. st. p. n. e., što potvrđuje ljudsku prisutnost na platou Ravna za vrijeme završne faze brončanog doba.

*

Treće nalazište na kojem su sprovedena arheološka iskopavanja u 2019. godini je visinsko naselje Kopilo sa kojeg se kontrolira ulazna dionica rijeke Bosne kao i veći dio Zeničkog bazena. Ovo uzvišenje je sa tri strane zaštićeno strmim stranama a kao naseobinski prostor ističu se najviši, bedemom ograđeni plato te dvije terase koje se pružaju smjeru zapada. Na Kopilu su već

and offers room for settling and human activity on the highest plateau, fortified by a mighty rampart and two adjoining terraces to the west side. This site was the object of previous excavations that yielded characteristic Bronze and Iron Age pottery and pieces of iron slag, but gave little information on structures within the settlement. The plateau near the top of the hill was chosen for the new excavation because it is closed off from the lower plateau by a steep slope and a rampart, which provides additional security. This advantage is reflected in the multiphase settlement remains that were documented. Iron Age contexts from the time between the 6th and the 2nd centuries BC and objects from the domestic sphere including loom weights, stone tools, numerous pottery sherds and iron objects and semi-finished products, which indicate the existence of an early domestic iron metallurgy, were unearthed in Trench 3. The highlight among the new finds is a male figurine made of clay, which stands out as a singular find in its time in central Bosnia without exact analogies. Time ran out, so the Bronze Age layers below await excavation in the future. Mixed contexts from Trench 1 yielded plenty of Bronze Age pottery as well as finds pointing to occupation during the 3rd and 2nd centuries BC (wheel-made pottery and a bronze fibula), which proves settlement continuity of over a thousand years at Kopilo and underlines the importance of the site within the micro-region of the Zenica Basin of the Bosna River.

Summary and Outlook

The research activities in the Zenica Basin over the past three years have contributed significantly to our knowledge of this mountainous Balkan region's prehistory. For the 2019 excavations, three areas of interest were selected – two hilltop settlements (Kopilo and Ravna) and a group of stone tumuli at Gradišće.

For Kopilo, a Bronze Age and Iron Age presence can be established. A C14 date from Ravna proves 12th century BCE activity in the area, which falls into the end stage of the Bronze Age. The two excavated stone tumuli at Gradišće were disturbed in earlier times but they are the first to be documented scientifically in the region and are most probably from the Bronze Age too. The airborne laser scans of Kopilo and Gradišće revealed various traces of human activity through time and highlight the potential for future research. Continuation of the excavations at Kopilo and in Gradišće in the coming years is planned.

vršena manja arheološka iskopavanja u kojima je pronađena karakteristična keramika brončanog i željeznog doba kao i komadi željezne troske, no informacije o strukturi naselja ne postoje.

Nova iskopavanja sprovedena su na najvišem platou koji predstavlja jasno izdvojen dio naseobinskog kompleksa sa strmim prijelazom i bedemom kao dodatnim utvrđenjem prema susjednim terasama na zapadu. U iskopavanjima su dokumentirani ostaci naseljavanja iz više perioda koji svjedoče o dugotrajnom životu na ovom mjestu. U sondi 3 otkriveni su ostaci objekata iz željeznog doba odnosno iz vremena između 6. i 2. st. p. n. e. kao i brojni pripadajući pokretni nalazi uključujući mnoštvo keramičkih posuda, tegova za tkalački stan, kamenih alatki, željeznih predmeta i polufinalnih metalnih poizvoda koji su ujedno izravan dokaz o postojanju metalurgije unutar naselja. Vrijedi svakako istaknuti i pronalazak jedne glinene figurine sa predstavom muškog lika koja je zasada jedinstven nalaz u regiji centralne Bosne bez odgovarajućih analogija. Iskopavanja su okončana dostizanjem slojeva željeznog doba a dublji i stariji slojevi brončanodobnog naselja biti će istraženi u bliskoj budućnosti. U sondi 1 pronađen je veliki broj brončanodobne keramike, nažalost u sekundarnom položaju i poremećenom kontekstu, kao i određeni broj nalaza karakterističnih za period 3. i 2. st. p. n. e. (keramika rađena na vitlu i jedna brončana fibula). I ovi nalazi dokaz su izrazitog kontinuiteta na Kopilu kao mjesta koje je preko 1000 godina predstavljalo jedno od ključnih naselja u ovoj specifičnoj mikroregiji u dolini rijeke Bosne.

Zaključak i perspektiva

Istraživanja u zadnje tri godine značajano su pridonijela boljem sagledavanju prahistorije u ovom planinskom predjelu Balkana. Iskopavanja u 2019. godini koncentrirala su se na dva visinska naselja (Kopilo i Ravna) i grupu kamenih humki iznad Gradišća.

U slučaju Kopila nedvojben je kontinuitet naseljavanja kroz brončano i željezno doba. Radiokarbonski datumi sa platoa Ravna ukazuju na aktivnosti u toku 12. st. p. n. e. odnosno u vrijeme završne faze brončanog doba. Ispitani kameni tumuli iznad Gradišća već su u prahistorijsko vrijeme značajno poremećeni, no radi se prvim takvim nalazima u centranoj Bosni koji su dokumentirani naučnim metodama i koji najvjerovatnije potječu iz brončanog doba.

Digitalni topografski modeli prostora oko naselja Kopilo i duž sedlastog grebena iznad Gradišća ukazali su na prisutnost raznih tragova ljudske aktivnosti kroz duži vremenski period a ujedno i naznačili veliki potencijal budućih istraživanja. U slijedećim godinama, arheološka iskopavanja predviđena su na nalazištima Kopilo i Gradišće.

GLOSSARY

REČNIK TERMINA

Barbara Horejs / Mario Gavranović / Clare Burke / Bogdana Milić /
Michael Brandl / Irene M. Petschko

– A –

aDNA – short for "ancient deoxyribonucleic acid", which carries the genetic information of past populations

Airborne scanning (LiDAR) – a prospection method used to detect traces of human activity in areas under vegetation

Anthropological analyses – analyses of preserved human remains in order to identify the age, sex, possible diseases and other characteristics

Anthropomorphic – creatures or objects that have human characteristics and can be assigned human emotions and physical attributes

Archaeological survey – a method of non-intrusive field research for identifying archaeological sites and collecting information about the location, distribution and organization of past human communities

Archaeometallurgist – an expert in ancient metals and metal production

– B –

Bronze Age – the period between 2300 and 900 BC in southeast Europe named after the copper alloy with tin

Bier – a wooden frame construction on which the deceased was placed

– C –

Caričin Grad (Justiniana Prima) – Byzantine city (AD 535–615) in the Lebane district, founded by the Emperor Justinian I (AD 527–565)

Chaff – dry remains of cereals and other plants

Chalcedony – pale bluish quartz variety with similar properties to chert, but no fossil inclusions

Chert – a variety of quartz, containing microfossils, that breaks with sharp edges

Chipped stone tools – before metal was known, rocks which break like glass were skilfully cracked (chipped) to produce implements for which sharp edges were required

Composite tools – a tool that is composed of multiple pieces inserted into a handle

Core drilling – a geoarchaeological method to detect and sample subsurface geological and/or anthropogenic archives

Cremation remains – burned human bones, usually deposited in a ceramic container (urn)

– D –

Digital elevation model – the outcome of airborne scanning showing the contours of the terrain without vegetation

– E –

Eneolithic/Copper Age – the period characterized by the use of copper, c. 4500–2300 BC in southeast Europe

– F –

Fibula – a decorative brooch for fastening clothes

Figurine – a miniature sculpture representing a human or animal

– G –

Geoarchaeology – a discipline based on geology, archaeology, geography and general Earth sciences

Geophysical surveys – non-destructive ground-based physical sensing techniques used for imaging subsurface archaeological features

– H –

Hilltop settlement – a settlement situated on higher ground. If it is protected by fortifications (ramparts, ditches), it is also called a hillfort

– I –

Imagery – the use of pictures to create images, esp. to create an impression or mood (after Cambridge Dictionary – https://dictionary.cambridge.org/de/worterbuch/englisch/imagery [23.6.2020])

Iron Age – the period between c. 900 and the Roman conquests in southeast Europe. Characterized by the first introduction of iron technology

– J –

Jasper – a colourful quartz variety with similar properties to chert, but no fossil inclusions

– K –

Knapping techniques – techniques employed to shape raw materials which have specific fracturing features in order to produce stone tools

– L –

Lithic – relating to stone

Loom weights – ceramic objects made in order to tauten the threads of the loom

– M –

Macroscopic analysis – examining what is visible to the eye without magnification or equipment

Metallic slag – waste product of ore processing and metal extraction

Microscopic analysis – examining material using a high magnification microscope that allows small inclusions to be clearly visible

– N –

Neolithic – New Stone Age, the period between c. 6000 and 4500 BC in the Balkans

Neolithization – the process of the distribution of the main components of the Neolithic period, such as sedentism, farming and herding as the new means of economic subsistence, new production technologies and new material culture (e.g. ceramic vessel production, polished stone implements)

– P –

Pedology – scientific discipline describing the study of soils in their natural environment

Percussion – a technique used in the production of stone tools, involving striking, hitting or breaking with a soft or hard hammer (antler, wood or stone), either through direct application (direct percussion) or with an intermediary object (indirect percussion)

Pottery Fabric – the combination of clay and rock inclusions that are used to make ceramics

– R –

Radiocarbon dating – a method for determining the age of organic material by using the properties/radioactive decay of the carbon isotope C14

Refining – extraction of impurities from the metal, last step of metal production from the ore

Retouch – secondary modification made by removing small flakes in order to blunt, sharpen or refine the outline or prepare the edge of the tool

– S –

Silica sheen – a polished (wax-like) shiny surface on the edge of a blade or flake suggesting that the tool was used to cut grass or cereals rich in silica

Spindle whorl – a spherical or cylindrical object used in the process of spinning and coiling the spun thread

Starčevo – archaeological site, toponymal for the early to middle Neolithic period in the central Balkans between c. 6000 and 5300 BC

– T –

Trace elements – chemical elements with very low concentrations (e.g. in rocks or metals)

Tumulus – a human-made mound

– V –

Vinča culture – the main late Neolithic and Early Copper Age cultural manifestation in the central Balkans, named after the Vinča site near Belgrade

– W –

Wattle and daub technique – construction method for walls and buildings using wooden strips ('wattle') and an adhesive material such as soil, clay, dung or straw ('daub')

Wheel-made pottery – pottery made with the help of a wheel, introduced in the Balkans in the younger stage of the Iron Age (c. 5th century BC). Before that, all pottery was made using the hand-building technique.

– A –

Alatke od okresanog kamena – pre upotrebe metala, različite kamene sirovine su se obrađivale cepanjem (okresivanjem) kako bi se dobile alatke oštrih ivica

Antička DNK – skraćenica za „drevnu deoksiribonukleinsku kiselinu", koja sadrži genetske informacije drevnih populacija

Antropološke analize – analize očuvanih ljudskih ostataka radi identifikacije

Antropomorfno – predmeti koja imaju ljudske karakteristike i na kojima se mogu prepoznati emocije i fizička svojstva

Arheološko rekognosciranje – metoda nedestruktivnog terenskog istraživanja u cilju identifikacije arheoloških nalazišta i prikupljanja podataka o lokaciji, rasprostranjenosti i organizaciji ljudskih zajednica u prošlosti

Arheometalurg – stručnjak za drevne metale i proizvodnju metala

– B –

Bronzano doba – period između 2300. i 900. godine prije nove ere u jugoistočnoj Evropi, nazvan po leguri bakra sa kositrom/kalajem

– C –

Caričin Grad (Justiniana Prima) – vizantijski grad (535–615. godine nove ere) u okrugu Lebana, koji je osnovao car Justinijan I (527–565. godine nove ere)

– D –

Digitalni visinski model – rezultat skeniranja iz zraka koje pokazuje konture terena bez vegetacije

– E –

Eneolit/ bakarno doba – period za koji je karakteristična upotreba metala bakra, ca. 4500–2300. pre nove ere u jugoistočnoj Evropi

– F –

Fibula – dekorativni broš za pričvršćivanje odjeće/tkanine

Figurina – minijaturna skulptura ljudskog ili životinjskog lika

– G –

Geoarheologija – disciplina zasnovana na geologiji, arheologiji, geografiji i opštim naukama o zemlji

Geofizička rekognosciranja –- nedestruktivne metode senzorske prospekcije koje se koriste za snimanje arheoloških struktura pod zemljom

– J –

Jaspis – vrsta kvarca u boji, sličnih karakteristika kao rožnac koji ne sadrži mikrofosile

– K –

Kalcedon – bledoplava vrsta kvacra sličnih karakteristika kao rožnac, ne sadrži mikrofosile

Keramika na vitlu – keramika proizvedena uz pomoć vitla, uvedena na Balkanu sa mlađom fazom gvozdenog doba (oko 5. veka pre nove ere). Pre toga, sav keramički materijal izrađivan je ručnom tehnikom

Kompozitne alatke – alatke koja se sastoji od više komada umetnutih u dršku

– L –

Lasersko skeniranje iz zraka (LiDAR) – metoda prospekcije koja se koristi za otkrivanje tragova ljudskih aktivnosti u prostoru pod gustom vegetacijom

Litički – odnosi se na kamen, izrađeno od kamena, u osnovi kamen

– M –

Makroskopska analiza – ispitivanje onoga što je očima vidljivo bez uvećanja ili opreme

Metalna šljaka – otpadni proizvod prerade rude i ekstrakcije metala

Mikroskopska analiza – ispitivanje materijala pomoću mikroskopa visokog uvećanja koji omogućava da vidljivost malih inkluzija

Nečistoće – niske koncentracije određenih hemijskih elemenata (npr. u stenama ili u metalu)

– N –

Neolit – novo kameno doba, period između oko 6000. i 4500. godine pre nove ere na Balkanu

Neolitizacija – proces distribucije glavnih komponenti neolitskog perioda, kao što su sedentizam, poljoprivreda i stočarstvo kao osnova ekonomije i opstanka. Uvođenje novih tehnologije proizvodnje i nove materijalne kulture (npr. proizvodnja keramičkih posuda, poliranih kamenih alatki)

Nosila – drvena konstrukcija za prenos pokojnika

– O –

Ostaci kremiranja – spaljene ljudske kosti, obično deponovane u keramičkoj posudi (urni)

– P –

Pedologija – naučna disciplina koja se odnosi na proučavanje tla u njihovom prirodnom okruženju

Perkusija – tehnika koja se koristi u proizvodnji kamenog alata, koja uključuje udaranje i prelom mekim ili tvrdim čekićem (rog, drvo ili kamen) bilo direktnom primenom (direktno udaranje) ili posredničkim predmetom (indirektno udaranje)

Pleva – suvi ostaci žitarica i drugih biljaka

Pršljenak – sferni ili cilindrični predmet koji se koristi za predenje i namotavanje niti

– R –

Radiokarbonsko datiranje – metoda za određivanje starosti organskog materijala uz pomoć pravilnog raspada radioaktivnog ugljenikovog izotopa C14

Rafinacija – ekstrakcija nečistoća iz metala, posljednji korak pri dobijanju metala iz rude

Retuširanje – sekundarna modifikacija koja se odnosi na uklanjanje malih odbitaka da bi se kontura ili ivica alatke namerno istupila, naoštrila ili popravila

Rožnac – vrsta kvarca koja cepanjem obrazuje oštre ivice, sadrži mikrofosile

– S –

Sastav keramike – kombinacija dodataka/inkluzija u vidu gline i stena koji se koriste za izradu keramike

Silikatni sjaj – polirana (poput voska) sjajna površina na ivici sečiva ili odbitka, što sugeriše da je alatka korištena za sečenje trave ili žitarica bogatih silicijumom

Slikovno predstavljanje – upotreba slika za kreiranje predstava, naročito da bi se stvorio utisak ili raspoloženje (after Cambridge dictionary – https://dictionary.cambridge.org/de/worterbuch/englisch/imagery [23.6.2020])

Sondažno bušenje – geoarheološka metoda otkrivanja i uzorkovanja podzemnih geoloških i / ili antropogenih profila

Starčevo – toponimno arheološko nalazište ranog-srednjeg neolita na centralnom Balkanu između oko 6000. i 5300. godine pre nove ere

– T –

Tegovi za tkalački stan – keramički predmeti napravljeni da bi se zategli navoji tkalački stan

Tehnika pletera i lepa – način gradnje zidova i objekata upotrebom drvenih traka ("pleter") i lepljivog materijala kao što su zemlja, glina, balega, blato, slama ("lep")

Tehnike okresivanja – tehnike koje se koriste za oblikovanje sirovina sa specifičnim karakteristikama preloma u cilju proizvodnje kamenih alatki

Tumul – humka, gomila napravljena odnosno nasuta ljudskom rukom

– V –

Vinčanska kultura – glavna manifestacija kasnog neolita i ranog bakarnog doba na centralnom Balkanu, nazvana po lokalitetu Vinča kod Beograda

Visinsko utvrđeno naselje – naselje koje se nalazi na višoj poziciji, obično zaštićeno utvrđenjima (bedemi, jarci)

– Ž –

Željezno doba – period između otprilike 900. godine i rimskih osvajanja u jugoistočnoj Evropi, karakteriziran uvođenjem tehnologije željeza

FIGURES/PHOTOS

ILUSTRACIJE/FOTOGRAFIJE

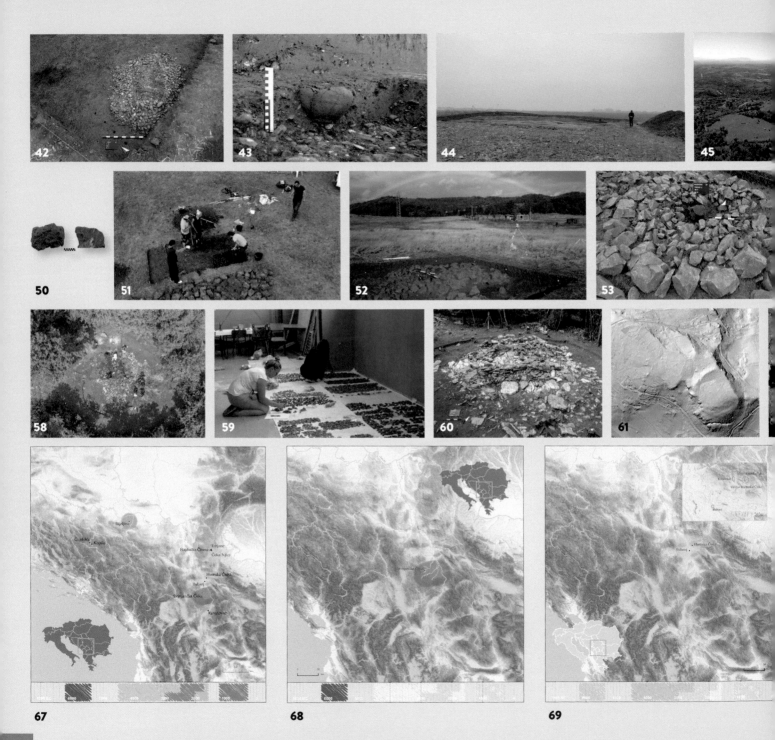

42

43

44

45

50

51

52

53

58

59

60

61

67

68

69

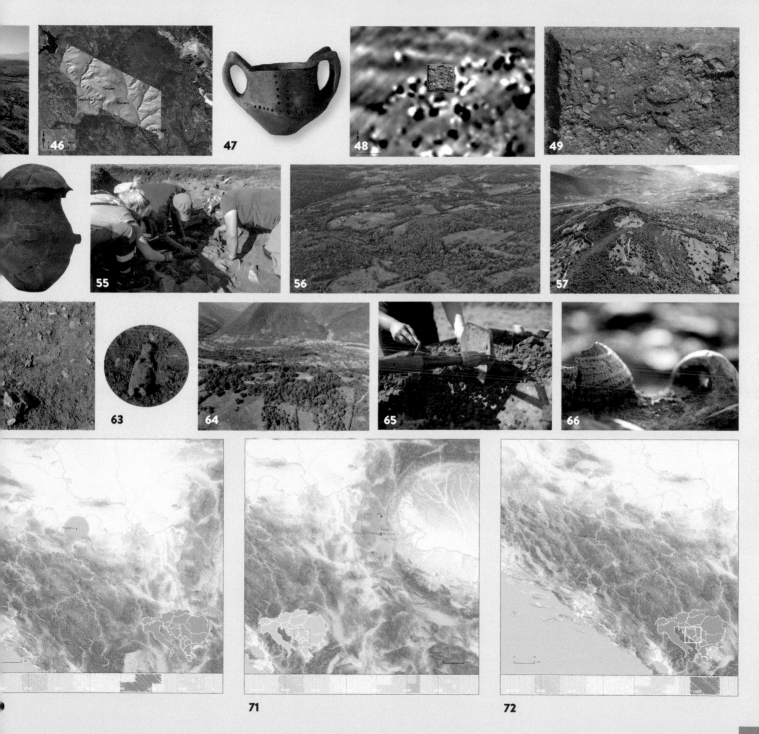

46   47   48   49

55   56   57

63   64   65   66

71   72

Photo credits / izvori fotografija

Cover/Naslovnica   Northern Trench of Svinjarička Čuka / Naslovna strana: Severna sonda na lokalitetu Svinjarička Čuka (photo/fotografija: F. Ostmann)

1. Surface finds collected at Svinjarička Čuka during the survey / Površinski nalazi prikupljeni sa Svinjaričke Čuke u toku rekognosciranja (photo/fotografija: F. Ostmann)

2. Jablanica River near Lebane / Reka Jablanica u blizini Lebana (photo/fotografija: F. Ostmann)

3. Southern Trench of Svinjarička Čuka / Južna sonda na lokalitetu Svinjarička Čuka (photo/fotografija: F. Ostmann)

4. South Morava River / Južna Morava (photo/fotografija: M. Boerner)

5. Core Drilling / Sondažno bušenje (photo/fotografija: F. Ostmann)

6. Geophysical Survey / Geofizičko rekognosciranje (photo/fotografija: Eastern Atlas)

7. Drone in use for orthogonal photography / Korišćenje drone u ortogonalnom snimanju (photo/fotografija: F. Ostmann)

8. River terrace at Svinjarička Čuka / Rečna terasa na Svinjaričkoj Čuki (photo/fotografija: M. Boerner)

9. Stone axe in situ within a Neolithic structure / In situ kamena sekira iz neolitskog objekta (photo/fotografija: F. Ostmann)

10. Burnt daub of a Neolithic structure / Goreli lep iz neolitskog objekta (photo/fotografija: F. Ostmann)

11. Macroscopic and microscopic representation of lithic raw materials from the Svinjarička River / Makroskopski i mikroskopski prikaz kamenih sirovina iz Svinjaričke reke (photo/fotografija: M. Brandl)

12. Primary chalcedony outcrop at the village of Bučumet–Kameno Rebro / Primarno ležište kalcedona u selu Bučumet-Kameno Rebro (photo/fotografija: M. Brandl)

13. Gravels of the Svinjarička River / Šljunak Svinjaričke reke (photo/fotografija: M. Brandl)

14. Tools and cores (local and exotic raw materials) from the Neolithic Svinjarička Čuka / Alatke i jezgra od okresanog kamena (lokalni i egzotični materijali) sa Svinjaričke Čuke (photos/fotografije: F. Ostmann)

15. Collection of retouched tools from the Neolithic Svinjarička Čuka / Kolekcija retuširanih alatki sa neolitskog lokaliteta Svinjarička Čuka (photos/fotografije: F. Ostmann)

16. Bowl, Starčevo type / Zdela starčevačkog tipa (photo/fotografija: F. Ostmann)

17. Pottery processing in the "sherd yard" / Obrada keramike u "bašti ulomaka" (photo/fotografija: F. Ostmann)

18. Microscopic analysis in the OREA Raw Material Lab / Mikroskopske analize u OREA Raw Material laboratoriji (photo/fotografija: F. Ostmann)

19. Cross section of pottery sherd break / Presek keramičkog ulomka (photo/fotografija: F. Ostmann)

20. Biconical bowl, classical Starčevo type / Bikonična zdela klasično starčevačkog tipa (photo/fotografija: F. Ostmann)

21. Finger impressions on the inside of a vessel / Otisci prstiju u unutrašnjosti posude (photo/fotografija: F. Ostmann)

22. 3D scan of finger impressions on the inside of a vessel / 3D sken otisaka prstiju iz unutrašnjosti posude (digital model/digitalni model: I. Petschko)

23. Anthropomorphic Figurines / Antropomorfne figurine (photo/fotografija: F. Ostmann)

24. Zoomorphic Figurine / Zoomorfna figurina (photo/fotografija: F. Ostmann)

25. Parts of a ceramic vessel found during excavations / Delovi keramičke posude sa iskopavanja (photo/fotografija: F. Ostmann)

26. Aerial view of the site Velika Humska Čuka / Lokalitet Velika Humska Čuka, snimak dronom sa istoka (photo/fotografija: A. Bulatović)

27. The mutual position of sites Velika Humska Čuka, Mala Humska Čuka, Kremenac and Bubanj, drone shot from the north / Međusobni položaj lokaliteta Velika humska čuka, Mala humska čuka, Kremenac i Bubanj, snimak dronom sa severa (photo/fotografija: A. Bulatović)

28. Possible reconstruction of House 1 / Moguća rekonstrukcija kuće 1 (A. Bulatović, A. Kapuran)

29. Remains of House 1 with floor and five vessels in a row, in situ, shot from the east / Ostaci kuće 1 sa podnicom i pet posuda u nizu, in situ, snimak sa istoka (photo/foto: A. Bulatović)

30. A portion of the inventory of House 3 / Deo inventara kuće 3 (photo/fotografija: A. Bulatović)

31. A pit buried into the floor of House 3, shot from the south / Jama ukopana u podnicu kuće 3, snimak sa juga (photo/foto: A. Bulatović)

32. Pottery fragment with gold coating from House 3 and a detail of golden coating/ Fragment keramike iz kuće 3 sa zlatnom prevlakom i detalj zlatne prevlake (photo/fotografija: A. Bulatović)

33. Velika Humska Čuka, excavation 2017 / Velika humska čuka, iskopavanja 2017. Godine (photo/fotografija: A. Bulatović)

34. Fragments of painted pottery from the Classical Greek Period (4* century BC) / Fragmenti slikane keramike iz perioda klasične Grčke (IV vek pre n.e.) (photo/fotografija: A. Bulatović)

35. Aerial view of the site Novo Selo near Bijeljina from the north / Lokalitet Novo selo, snimak dronom sa sjevera (photo/fotografija: M. Börner)

36. Geophysical survey of two tumuli near Bijeljina / Geofizička prospekcija tumula kod Bijeljine (photo/fotografija: M. Gavranović)

37. Digital elevation model of the site Novo Selo with newly discovered second elevation / Visinski model nalazišta Novo Selo sa drugim uzvišenjem pored tumula (DEM: I. Petschko; drone photography for 3D: M. Börner)

38. Visualization of the geophysical data from the site Novo Selo on drone footage / Vizualizacija geofizičkih rezultata na snimku terena iz drona (geophysical data: Eastern Atlas; photo/foto: M. Börner)

39. Aerial view of the site Novo Selo near Bijeljina / Lokalitet Novo selo, snimak dronom (photo/fotografija: M. Börner)

40. Documentation of medieval tombs at the site Novo Selo / Dokumentacija srednjovjekovnih grobova na lokalitetu Novo Selo (photo/foto: M. Gavranović)

41. Excavation of the Middle Bronze Age tomb at the site Novo Selo / Iskopavanje groba is srednjeg bronzanog doba na nalazištu Novo Selo (photo/fotografija: M. Börner)

42. Middle Bronze Age burial on a stone platform, which was covered by the tumulus at the site Novo Selo / Grob iz srednjeg bronzanog doba na kamenoj platformi iznad kojeg je podignut tumul na lokalitetu Novo Selo (photo/fotografija: M. Gavranović)

43. Copper Age urn burial at the site Novo Selo / Urna sa kremiranim ljudskim ostacima iz bakarnog doba na nalazištu Novo Selo (photo/fotografija: M. Gavranović)

44. View on the excavation of the tumulus at the site Novo Selo / Pogled na iskopavanja tumula u Novom Selu (photo/fotografija: M. Gavranović)

45. The site Čoka Njica, drone shot from the East/ Lokalitet Čoka Njica, snimak dronom sa istoka (photo/fotografija: T. Urban)

46. Digital elevation model created with the project's airborne laser scan (LiDAR) data and location of the four sites west of Bor / Digitalni visinski model dobiven skeniranjem terena iz vazduha LiDAR tehnikom u okviru projekta sa četiri lokaliteta zapadno d grada Bora (map background/karta u pozadini: Microsoft Bing)

47. Vatin beaker found at the site Trnjane / Pehar vatinskog tipa pronađen na lokalitetu Trnjane (photo/fotografija: T. Urban)

48. Four urn burials in circular stone structures excavated at the site Hajdučka Česma in 2018 on the visualization of the geophysical survey of the urn cemetery / Četiri groba sa urnama i kružnim kamenim konstrukcijama otkrivena 2018. godine na lokalitetu Hajdučka Česma. U pozadini je snimka geofizičke prospekecije na nekrpoli (orthophoto/ortofoto: I. Petschko; data for 3D photogrammetry/snimci za 3D fotogrametriju: T. Urban; geophysical data/geofizički snimak: Eastern Atlas)

49. Copper ore smelting installation at the site Čoka Njica / Ostaci peći za preradu bakarne rude na nalazišti Čoka Njica (photo/fotografija: T. Urban)

50. Metallic slag from the site Trnjane / Metalična šljaka sa lokaliteta Trnjane (photo/fotografija: M. Mehofer; copyright: University of Vienna)

51. Excavation at the site Čoka Njica in 2019 / Iskopavanja na lokalitetu Čoka Njica u 2019. godini (photo/fotografija: T. Urban)

52. Excavation at the site Hajdučka Česma in 2018 / Iskopavanja na lokalitetu Hajdučka Česma u 2018. godini (photo/fotografija: T. Urban)

53. Urn burial 2, excavated at the site Hajdučka Česma in 2018 / Grob 2, urna sa kružnom kamenom konstrukcijom na lokalitetu Hajdučka Česma (photo/fotografija: M. Gavranović)

54. Urn with lid, Grave 1, Hajdučka Česma / Urna sa poklopcem, grob 1, Hajdučka Česma (photo/fotografija: M. Gavranović)

55. Excavation of Grave 5, Hajdučka Česma 2019 / Iskopavanje groba 5, Hajdučka Česma (photo/fotografija: T. Urban)

56. Aerial view of the sites Trnjane and Hajdučka Česma / Lokaliteti Trnjane i Hajdučka Česma, snimak dronom sa istoka (photo/fotografija: T. Urban)

57. The hill chain upon Gradišće overlooking the Zenica basin / Vijenac uzvišenja iznad Gradišća i pogled na Zenički bazen (photo/fotografija: T. Urban)

58. Excavation of stone tumulus 1 at the site Gradišće in 2019 / Iskopavanja kamenog tumula 1 na lokalitetu Gradišće u 2019. godini (photo/fotografija: T. Urban)

59. Processing the pottery found during the excavation at the site Kopilo / Obrada keramičkih nalaza pronađenih na lokalitetu Kopilo u toku iskopavanja u 2019. godini (photo/fotografija: I. Petschko)

60. Stone structure in the center of tumulus 1 at the site Gradišće / Kamena konstrukcija u centralnom dijelu tumula 1 na lokalitetu Gradišće (photo/fotografija: M. Gavranović)

61. Digital elevation model of the hilltop settlement Kopilo created with the project's airborne laser scan data / Digitalni visinski model visinskog naselja Kopilo dobiven skeniranjem terena iz zraka LiDAR tehnikom u okviru projekta

62. Male clay figurine in the find context at the site Kopilo / Glinena figurina muškarca na mjestu nalaza na lokalitetu Kopilo (photo/fotografija: T. Urban)

63. Male clay figurine found at Kopilo / Glinena figurina muškarca, Kopilo (photo/fotografija: T. Urban)

64. The plateau of the hilltop settlement site Ravna overlooking the river Bosna and the Zenica basin entrance from the North / Plato visinskog naselja Ravna sa rijekom Bosnom u pozadini i ulazom u Zenički bazen iz pravca sjevera (photo/fotografija: T. Urban)

65. Sieving to revover small objects at Svinjarička Čuka / Prosejavanje u cilju pronalaženja sitnih nalaza na Svinjaričkoj Čuki (photo/fotografija: F. Ostmann)

66. Fragmented ceramic pots on a Bronze Age floor / Fragmentovane keramičke posude na bronzanodopskoj podnici (photo/fotografija: F. Ostmann)

67. The five case study areas and the timeline of Visualizing the Unknown Balkans / Pet regionalnih studija i vremenski okvir nalazišta uključenih u projekt Vizualizacija nepoznatog Balkana (design/dizajn: I. Petschko; map background/karta u pozadini: MeritDEM, Open Street Map, Natural Earth, Eurostat)

68. Location and timeline of the case study area First farmers and herders in South Serbia / Pozicija i vremenski okvir regionale studije Prvi zemljoradnici i stočari u Južnoj Srbiji (design/dizajn: I. Petschko; map background/karta u pozadini: MeritDEM, Open Street Map, Natural Earth, Eurostat)

69. Location and timeline of the case study area The rising of Copper Age central places / Pozicija i vremenski okvir regionale studije Uspon centralnih mesta bakarnog doba (design/dizajn: I. Petschko; map background/karta u pozadini: MeritDEM, ALOS DEM, Open Street Map, Natural Earth, Eurostat)

70. Location and timeline of the case study area Prehistoric burial mounds (tumuli) in northeastern Bosnia / Pozicija i vremenski okvir regionale studije Praistorijske grobne humke (tumuli) u sjeveroistočnoj Bosni (design/dizajn: I. Petschko; map background/karta u pozadini: MeritDEM, Open Street Map, Natural Earth, Eurostat)

71. Location and timeline of the case study area Bronze Age metallurgy in East Serbia / Pozicija i vremenski okvir regionale studije Bronzanodobna metalurgija u istočnoj Srbiji (design/dizajn: I. Petschko; map background/karta u pozadini: MeritDEM, Open Street Map, Natural Earth, Eurostat)

72. Location and timeline of the case study area Bronze Age communities in central Bosnia / Pozicija i vremenski okvir regionale studije Brončano doba u srednjoj Bosni (design/dizajn: I. Petschko; map background/karta u pozadini: MeritDEM, Open Street Map, Natural Earth, Eurostat)

Introductory Literature / Uvodna literatura

D. W. Bailey, Prehistoric figurines: representation and corporeality in the Neolithic. London – New York 2005.

E. Bánffy, First farmers of the Carpathian basin: changing patterns in subsistence, ritual and monumental figurines. Prehistoric Society Research Papers 8, Oxford 2019.

M. Bogdanović, 2008. Grivac: settlements of the Proto-Starčevo and Vinča culture. Kragujevac 2008.

V. Bogosavljević Petrović, A. Starović, The context of the Early Neolithic in Serbia: hidden reflections of Mesolithic continuity?, Glasnik Glasnik Srpskog arheološkog društva 32, 2015, 7–50.

M. Brandl, The multi layered chert sourcing approach (MLA). Analytical provenance studies of silicite raw materials, Archeometriai Műhely 13/3, 2016, 145–156.

M. Brandl, C. Hauzenberger, Geochemical sourcing of lithic raw materials from secondary deposits in south Serbia: Implications for early Neolithic resource management strategies, Archaeologia Austriaca 102, 2018, 55–70.

E. Bujak, History of Gradišče from prehistory to the end of Middle Ages. Gradina 1, Zenica 2012, 9–32.

A. Bulatović, Relations between cultural groups in the Early Bronze Age in South-eastern Serbia, Western Bulgaria and North-eastern Macedonia, Archaeologia Bulgarica 15/2, 2011, 81–94.

A. Bulatović, J. Stankovski, Bronzano doba u basenu Južne Morave i u dolini Pčinje. Belgrade – Kumanovo 2012.

A. Bulatović, D. Milanović, Velika humska čuka, istraživanja 2009. godine: prilog proučavanju stratigrafije eneolita i bronzanog doba u jugoistočnoj Srbiji, Glasnik Srpskog arheološkog društva 30, 2014, 163–188.

A. Bulatović, M. Gori, M. Vander Linden, New AMS dates as a contribution to the absolute chronology of the Early Eneolithic in the central Balkans, Starinar 68, 2018, 19–32.

A. Bulatović, M. Gavranović, A. Kapuran, New absolute dates for the Middle and Late Bronze Ages in central Balkans and some indications or the local metallurgy and workshops. In: R. Jung, H. Popov (eds.), Searching for Gold – Resources and Networks in the Bronze Age of the Eastern Balkans, forthcoming.

J. Chapman, The Vinča Culture of South-East Europe: Studies in Chronology, Economy and Society. British Archaeological Records International Series 117, Oxford 1981.

B. Čović, Uvod u stratigrafiju i hronologiju praistorijskih grrdina u Bosni, Glasnik Zemaljskog Muzeja u Sarajevu 20, 1965, 27–145.

B. Čović, Srednjobosanska kulturna grupa. In: A. Benac (ed.), Praistorija jugoslovenskih zemalja IV: Bronzano doba. Sarajevo 1983, 390–421.

B. Čović, Srednjobosanska grupa. In: A. Benac (ed.), Praistorija Jugoslovenskih Zemalja V: Željezno doba. Sarajevo 1987, 481–531.

S. Dimitrijević, Badenka kultura. In: A. Benac (ed.), Praistorija jugoslovenskih zemalja III: Eneolitsko doba. Sarajevo 1979, 183–235.

V. J. Fewkes, H. Goldman, R. W. Ehrich, Excavations at Starčevo, Yugoslavia: Seasons 1931 and 1932, Bulletin of the American School of Prehistoric Research 9, 1933, 33–55.

V. Fewkes, Archaeological reconnaissance in Yugoslavia, season 1933, Bulletin of the American school of prehistoric research 12, 1936, 31.

M. Garašanin, D. Garašanin, Nova iskopavanja na Velikoj Humskoj Čuki kod Niša, Starinar 9–10, 1959, 243–254.

M. Garašanin, Praistorija na tlu SR Srbije. Belgrade 1973.

M. Garašanin, N. Đurić, Bubanj i Velika humska čuka, Niš. Narodni muzej Niš. Niš 1983.

M. Garašanin, Paraćinska grupa. In: A. Benac (ed.), Praistorija jugoslovenskih zemalja IV: Bronzano Doba. Sarajevo 1983, 727–735.

M. Gavranović, Keramik mit Basarabi- und basarabiartiger Ornamentik in Bosnien, Godišnjak Centra za balkanološka ispitivanja 34, 2007, 35–67.

M. Gavranović, Die Spätbronze- und Früheisenzeit in Bosnien. Universitätsforschungen zur Prähistorischen Archäologie 195, Bonn 2011.

M. Gimbutas, Anza, ca. 6500–5000 B.C.: A cultural yardstick for the study of Neolithic southeast Europe, Journal of Field Archaeology 1/1, 1974, 26–66.

H. J. Greenfield, T. Jongsma Greenfield, S. Jezik, Subsistence and settlement in the early Neolithic of Temperate SE Europe: A view from Blagotin, Serbia, Archaeologia Bulgarica 18/1, 2014, 1–33.

M. Gurova, Chipped-stone assemblages from the prehistoric site of Drenovac (Serbia). In: S. Perić (ed.), The Neolithic in the Middle Morava Valley, Belgrade 2016, 29–58.

S. Hansen, Bilder vom Menschen der Steinzeit: Untersuchungen zur anthropomorphen Plastik der Jungsteinzeit und Kupferzeit in Südosteuropa. Archäologie in Eurasien 20, Mainz 2007.

B. Horejs, A. Bulatović, C. Meyer , B. Milić, S. Schneider, M. Schlöffel, V Stevanović, Prehistoric landscapes of the Pusta Reka region (Leskovac): New investigations along the southern Morava river, Glasnik 34, 2018, 23–51.

B. Horejs, A. Bulatović, Prvi rezultati arheoloških istraživanja lokaliteta Svinjarička Čuka kod Lebana / First results of the excavations at Svinjarička Čuka, Lebane, Leskovački Zbornik 59, 2019, 45–54.

B. Horejs, A. Bulatović, J. Bulatović, M. Brandl, C. Burke, D. Filipović, B. Milić, New insights into the later stage of the Neolithisation process of the central Balkans: First excavations at Svinjarička Čuka 2018, Archaeologia Austriaca 103, 2019, 175–266.

I. Janković , P. Bugarski, S. Janjić, Copper slag as evidence of smelting and casting of copper in the period of Late Bronze Age in the surrounding of Bor, Zbornik radova muzeja rudarstva i metalurgije u Boru 5/6, 1987/1990, 13–19.

R. Jelenković, D. Milovanović, D. Koželj, M. Banješević, The mineral resources of the Bor metallogenic zone: A review, Geologia Croatica 69/2, 2016, 143–155.

B. Jovanović, Primary copper mining and the production of copper. In: P. T. Craddock (ed.), Scientific studies in early mining and extractive metallurgy. London 1980, 31–38.

B. Jovanović, N. Janković, Nekropola paraćinske grupe u Trnjanima kod Brestovačke banje, Zbornik radova Muzeja rudarstva i metalurgije u Boru 5/6, 1990, 1–12.

B. Jovanović, I. Janković, Die Keramik der Nekropole der Paraćin-Kultur-Trnjane bei Bor. In: N. Tasić (ed.), The Yugoslav Danube Basin and the Neighbouring Regions in the 2nd Millenium B.C. Belgrade 1996, 185–200.

A. Kapuran, I. Jovanović, Ružana: New Bronze Age metallurgical Center in North Eastern Serbia. In: N. Štrbac, D. Živković, S. Nestorović (eds.), 45th International Conference on Mining and Metallurgy. Bor 2013, 831–834.

A. Kapuran, Prehistoric Sites in North-Eastern Serbia (from Early Neolithic until Roman conquest). Belgrade 2014.

A. Kapuran, D. Živković, N. Štrbac, New evidence for prehistoric copper metallurgy in the vicinity of Bor, Starinar 66, 2016, 173–191.

A. Kapuran, N. Miladinović-Radmilović, N. Vuković, Funerary Traditions of the Bronze Age Metallurgical Communities in the Iron Gates Hinterland. In: D. Ložnjak-Dizdar, M. Dizdar, (eds.), Late Urnfeld Culture Between the Southern Alps and the Danube, Zbornik Instituta za Arheologiju 9. Zagreb 2017, 133–143.

A. Kapuran, M. Gavranović, M. Mehofer, Bronze Age settlement and necropolis Trnjane near Bor: revision and new research results, Starinar 70, 2020, in press.

S. Karmanski, Donja Branjevina: a Neolithic settlement near Deronje in the Vojvodina (Serbia). Società per la Preistoria e Protostoria della regiona Friuli-Venezia Guilia, Quaderno 10, Museo Civico di Storia Naturale, Trieste 2005.

R. Krauß, E. Marinova, H. De Brue, B. Weninger, The Rapid Spread of Early Farming from the Aegean into the Balkans via the Sub-Mediterranean-Aegean Vegetation Zone, Quaternary International 496, 2017, 24–41.

M. Kosorić, Cultural, ethnical and chronological problems of the Illyrian necropolises in the Drina basin. Dissertationes et Monographiae 17, Belgrade 1976.

M. Lazić, The Bor area in the Bronze Age. In: M. Lazić (ed.), The Bor Area in Prehistory, Antiquity and the Middle Ages. Bor – Belgrade 2004, 102–128.

J. L. Manson, Approaches to Starčevo culture chronology. In: C. Bonsall, V. Boroneanț, I. Radovanović (eds.), The Iron Gates in Prehistory: New Perspectives. British Archaeological Reports International Series 1893, Oxford 2008, 89–101.

Z. Marić, Praistorijski nalazi i lokaliteti iz Triješnice i Dvorova kod Bijeljine, Članci i građa za kulturnu istoriju istočne Bosne 1, 1961, 44–57.

M. Marić, Zaštitna arheološka istraživanja na lokaltietu Jaričište 1. In: V. Filipović, R. Arsić, D. Antonović (eds.), Rezultati novih arheoloških istraživanja u severozapadnoj Srbiji i susednim teritorijama. Belgrade 2013.

E. M. Marinova, D. Filipović, Đ. Obradović, E. Allue, Wild plant resources and land use in Mesolithic and Early Neolithic South-East Europe: archaeobotanical evidence from the Danube catchment of Bulgaria and Serbia, Offa 69/70, 2013, 467–478.

A. McPherron, D. Srejović, Divostin and the Neolithic of central Serbia. Ethnology Monographs 10, Kragujevac 1988.

V. Milojčić, Körös – Starčevo – Vinča. Mainz 1950.

O. Mladenović, B. Horejs, A. Bulatović, B. Milić, Austrijsko-srpski projekat Praistorijski pejzaži u regionu Puste reke (Leskovac) – istraživanja 2017. Godine. In: I. Bugarski, V. Filipović & N. Gavrilović Vitas (eds.), Arheologija u Srbiji. Projekti Arheološkog instituta u 2017. Godini, (Arheološki Institut), Beograd 2019.

J. Pavúk, Das balkanische Neolithikum als autonome Kultureinheit. In: Ü. Yalçin (ed.), Anatolian Metal VII: Anatolia and neighbours 10.000 years ago: Volume in honour of Mehmet Özdoğan. Anschnitt Beihefte 31, Bochum 2016, 233–254.

S. Perić, Der kulturelle Charakter und die Chronologie der Starčevo-Elemente im Neolithikum der westlichen Balkanregionen, Starinar 51, 2001, 9–39.

S. Perić, Topografija i kulturno-hronološke karakteristike naselja bronzanog i željeznog doba u gornjem toku reke Bosne. Zbornik za istoriju Bosne i Hercegovine 4, Belgrade 2004, 1–41.

S. Perić, The Oldest Cultural Horizon of Trench XV at Drenovac, Starinar 58, 2008, 29–50.

S. Perić (ed.), The Neolithic in the Middle Morava Valley: new insights into settlements and economy. Belgrade 2016.

E. Pernicka, F. Begemann, S. Schmitt-Strecker, G. A. Wagner, Eneolithic and Early Bronze Age Copper Artefacts from the Balkans and their Relation to Serbian Copper Ores, Praehistorische Zeitschrift 68, 1993, 1–54.

M. Porčić, T. Blagojević, S. Stefanović, Demography of the Early Neolithic population in Central Balkans: Population dynamics reconstruction using summed radiocarbon probability distributions, PLoS ONE 11/8, 2016, e0160832.

M. Radivojević, T. Rehren, E. Pernicka, D. Šljivar, M. Brauns, D. Borić, On the origins of extractive metallurgy: new evidence from Europe, Journal of Archaeological Science 37/11, 2010, 2775–2787.

J. Šarić, Early and middle Neolithic chipped stone artefacts from Serbia. Belgrade 2014.

S. Shennan, The first farmers of Europe: an evolutionary perspective. Cambridge 2018.

R. Šošić-Klindžić, The supply system of siliceous rocks between the Drava, Sava and Danube rivers during the Starčevo culture, Documenta Praehistorica 38, 2011, 345–356.

M. Spasić, The Vučedol period tumulus at the site of Batajnica-Velika Humska. In: P. Špehar, N. Strugar-Bevc (eds.), Batajnica-Velika Humska, Early Magyar Necropolis. Monografije 18, Muzej grada Beograda, Belgrade 2016, 162–176.

M. Stojić, Lieux de trouvaille de la céramique de type Vatin en Serbie au sud de la Save et du Danube. In: C. Schuster (ed.), Die Kulturen der Bronzezeit in dem Gebiet des Eisernen Tores. Kolloquium in Drobeta-Turnu Severin (November 1997). Bucarest 1998, 81–104.

D. Srejović, M. Lazić, Naselja i nekropole bronzanog doba u Timočkoj Krajini. In: M. Lazić (ed.) Arheologija istočne Srbije. Belgrade 1997, 225–247.

N. Tasić, Eneolithic cultures of Central and West Balkan. Belgrade 1995.

Č. Trajković, Kopilo, Zenica – praistrorijska gradina, Arheološki pregled 13, Belgrade 1971, 26–27.

R. Vasić, Cremation burials in the Morava valley between 1300 and 750 BC. In: M. Lochner, F. Ruppenstein (eds.), Cremation Burials in the Region between the Middle Danube and the Aegean, 1300–750 BC. Mitteilungen der Prähistorischen Kommission 77, Vienna 2013, 173–183.

Research Dissemination / Diseminacija istraživanja

Scientific publications / Stručne publikacije

M. Brandl, C. Hauzenberger, Geochemical sourcing of lithic raw materials from secondary deposits in south Serbia: Implications for early Neolithic resource management strategies, Archaeologia Austriaca 102, 2018, 55–70.

B. Horejs, C. Meyer, B. Milić, S. Schneider, M. Schlöffel, A. Bulatovic, Prehistoric Landscapes of the Pusta Reka Region (Lescovac). New Investigations along the southern Moravia River. Glasnik (Journal of Serbian Archaeological Society) 34, 2018, 23–51.

B. Horejs, A. Bulatović, J. Bulatović, M. Brandl, C. Burke, D. Filipović, B. Milić, New insights into the later stages of the Neolithisation process of the Central Balkans. First excavations at Svinjarička Čuka 2018. Archaeologia Austriaca 103, 2019, 175–226. doi: 10.1553/archaeologia103s175.

B. Horejs, A. Bulatović, B. Milić, O. Mladenović, Austrijsko-srpski projekat Praistorijski pejzaži u regionu Puste reke (Leskovac) – istraživanja 2017. godine. In: I. Bugarski, V. Filipović, N. Gavrilović Vitas (eds.), Arheologija u Srbiji. Projekti Arheološkog instituta u 2017. Godini, Belgrade 2019, 169–172.

B. Horejs, A. Bulatović, Prvi rezultati arheoloških istraživanja lokaliteta Svinjarička Čuka kod Lebana / First results of the excavations at Svinjarička Čuka, Lebane. Leskovački Zbornik 59, 2019, 45–54.

A. Kapuran, M. Gavranović, M. Mehofer, Bronze Age settlement and necropolis Trnjane near Bor: revision and new research results, Starinar 70, 2020, in press.

O. Mladenović, B. Horejs, A. Bulatović, B. Milić, Arheološka istraživanja na lokalitetu Svinjarička Čuka u 2018. i 2019. godini. In: S. Vitezović, Đ. Obradović, M. Radišić (eds.), Arheologija u Srbiji. Projekti Arheološkog instituta u 2019. Godini, Belgrade 2020.

Scientific Presentations / Stručna predavanja

J. Bulatović, D. Filipović, B. Horejs, Between the Mediterranean and temperate Europe: new evidence of Early Neolithic subsistence in southern Serbia. 1st conference on the Early Neolithic in Europe (ENE 2019) in Barcelona, Spain, 6th–8th November 2019.

M. Gavranović, A. Kapuran, M. Mehofer, New insights into Bronze Age metal production in Eastern Serbia – the copper smelting sites of Trnjane and Ružana. UK Gespräche - Bronze Age Metallurgy. Production – Consumption – Exchange. 23rd–24th May 2019, Institute OREA, Vienna, Austria, 23rd May 2019.

M. Gavranović, M. Mehofer, Metal consumption and exchange networks during the Bronze Age in the Western Balkans. UK Gespräche – Bronze Age Metallurgy. Production – Consumption – Exchange. 23rd–24th May 2019, Institute OREA, Vienna, Austria, 24th May 2019.

M. Gavranović, Higher ground – Choice, control and care. Bronze Age hilltop sites in central Bosnia. Archaeology of mountainous landscapes in Balkan Prehistory, 25th Annual Meeting of the European Association of Archeologists (EAA), 4th–7th September 2019, Bern, Switzerland, 5th September 2019.

M. Gavranović, First results of investigation in Hajdučka česma. International conference "Prehistoric communities along the Danube" in Osijek, Croatia, 29th November 2019.

M. Gavranović, I. Petschko, Revealing Bronze Age landscapes of the Balkans, 24th Conference of Cultural Heritage and New Technologies (CHNT), 4th–6th November 2019, Vienna, Austria, 4th November 2019.

M. Gavranović, Kupferproduktion in Ostserbien – Früh- bis Mittelbronzezeit. OREA Ausgrabungen 2019, Vienna, Austria, 11th December 2019.

B. Horejs, LBK & Vinča formation and transformation of Early Neolithic lifestyles in Europe in the second half of the 6th millennium BC. A southern perspective on the formation of early farming communities on the central Balkans, Tübingen, Germany, 22nd March 2019.

B. Horejs, Early farming communities between Anatolia, Aegean and the central Balkans, 1st conference on the Early Neolithic in Europe (ENE 2019) in Barcelona, Spain, 6th–8th November 2019.

B. Horejs, B. Milić, A. Bulatović, Trajectories of the Neolithic spread into the central Balkans. First results of new fieldwork in southern Serbia. 24th Neolithic Seminar Ljubljana, 26th–27th October 2018, Ljubljana, 26th October 2018.

B. Horejs, A southern perspective on the formation of early farming communities on the central Balkans. International Conference LBK & Vinča: Formation and Transformation of Early Neolithic Lifestyles in Europe in the second half of the 6th millennium BC. Tübingen, Germany, 22nd March 2019.

B. Milić, M. Brandl, K. Kotsakis, B. Horejs, Technological responses to raw materials in the Early Neolithic Aegean and the Balkans. 1st conference on the Early Neolithic in Europe (ENE 2019) in Barcelona, Spain. 6th–8th November 2019.

I. Petschko, M. Gavranović, Höhensiedlungen, Bosnien & Herzegowina – Spätbronzezeit und frühe Eisenzeit. OREA Ausgrabungen 2019, Vienna, Austria, 111th December 2019.

S. Schneider, M. Schlöffel, M. Brandl, C. Meyer, B. Milić, A. Bulatović, B. Horejs, Geoarchaeological investigations on the Neolithic landscapes of the Pusta Reka region in south-eastern Serbia, Arbeitskreis Geoarchäologie Jahrestagung in München: 4th–6th May 2018 (Poster presentation).

Organized workshops and sessions/ Radionice i sekcije

M. Gavranović, M. Mehofer, workshop: UK-Gespräche "Bronze Age Metallurgy: production – consumption – exchange", Vienna, Austria, 23rd–24th May 2019.

Public outreach / Javne prezentacije i popularizacija

The research activities enjoyed the attention of regional and national news outlets in Serbia and Bosnia and Herzegovina and beyond. TV interviews and reports were aired, newspaper articles online and offline were written.

M. Brandl, "Did we ever leave the Neolithic village? Lessons from Neolithic raw material economy", part of the lecture series "Archaeology of the Modern Era" at the Austrian embassy in Belgrade, Serbia, 3rd February 2020.

M. Gavranović, B. Horejs, Presentation of Visualizing the Unknown Balkans at the Austrian Embassy in Sarajevo, Bosnia to scientific colleagues from Bosnia and Serbia, 5th November 2018.

M. Gavranović, I. Petschko, engaged with the public at "Tag des Denkmals (Austrian Heritage Day) and premiered the pilot film for the project by 7Reasons, 30th September 2018.

M. Gavranović, I. Petschko, M. Konrad, M. Mehofer, Prähistorische Kupfergewinnung im serbischen Bor. Blog article in Austrian newspaper Der Standard, https://www.derstandard.at/story/2000112137007/praehistorische-kupfergewinnung-im-serbischen-bor [26.6.2020].

B. Horejs, "The transformation of Europeans into farmers. New research about the key role of the central Balkans 8000 years ago", first out of six lectures of the new lecture series "Archaeology of the Modern Era" at the Austrian embassy in Belgrade, Serbia, 12th September 2019.

B. Horejs, curation of the Neolithic part of the exhibition including objects from Svinjarička Čuka including a film about the research at Svinjarička Čuka (cut by I. Petschko) in the exhibition "Donau" at Schallaburg, Austria, 1st June–8th November 2020.

N. Mittermair, I. Petschko, M. Gavranović, Hoch hinaus in der Bronzezeit Zentralbosniens. Blog article in Austrian newspaper Der Standard, https://www.derstandard.at/story/2000109946934/hoch-hinaus-in-der-bronzezeit-zentralbosniens [26.6.2020].

The research at Svinjarička Čuka was presented at the Archaeology pavilion curated by B. Horejs at the "Be Open Science & Society" Festival in Vienna, 8th–12th September 2018.

In 2020 the results of the visualization work will be presented in collaboration with the Austrian Embassy in Belgrade to the scientific world and the interested public.

Funding

The project "Visualizing the Unknown Balkans" is funded by the Innovation Fund "Research, Science and Society" of the Austrian Academy of Sciences.

Principal investigators: Mario Gavranović & Barbara Horejs

Project team: Irene M. Petschko (project coordinator, research assistant), Bogdana Milić (PostDoc), Nicole Mittermair, Michael Konrad (student assistants)

Two project areas resulted in new projects funded by the Austrian Science Fund (FWF):

NEOTECH – Neolithic technological trajectories in the Balkans (FWF project no. P 32096)

Principal investigator: Barbara Horejs

New insights in Bronze Age metal producing societies (FWF project no. P 32095)

Principal investigator: Mario Gavranović

The project "Archaeological excavations at the site of Velika Humska Čuka in Hum near Niš" is financed by the Ministry of Culture and Information of the Republic of Serbia, the City of Niš and the Municipality of Crveni Krst in Niš. The project is realized by the Institute of Archaeology in Belgrade and the National Museum in Niš.

Project director : Aleksandar Bulatović

Project partner Aleksandar Kapuran received funding for parts of the 2019 excavations in Bor from the Ministry of Culture and Information, Republic of Serbia.

Izvori financija

Projekt "Vizualizacija nepoznatog Balkana" financiran je od strane Inovacijskog fonda "Istraživanje, nauka i društvo" Austrijske akademije nauka.

Voditelji projekta: Mario Gavranović & Barbara Horejs

Članovi projektnog tima: Irene M. Petschko (koordinacija projekta, naučni asistent), Bogdana Milić (PostDoc), Nicole Mittermair, Michael Konrad (studenti)

Dvije projektne studije rezultovale su pokretanjem novih istraživačkih projekata sa podrškom od strane Austrijskog naučnog fonda (FWF):

NEOTECH – Neolitski putevi tehnologije na Balkanu (FWF projekt br. P 32096)

Voditelj projekta: Barbara Horejs

Novi pogled na bronzanodobna društva i proizvodnju metala (FWF projekt br. P 32095)

Voditelj projekta: Mario Gavranović

Projekt "Arheološka iskopavanja na nalazištu Velika Humska Čuka u Humu kod Niša" financiran je od strane Ministarstva kulture i informacija Republike Srbije, grada Niša i opštine Crveni Krst u Nišu. Projekt je realizovan u saradnji Arheološkog Instituta u Beogradu i Narodnog muzeja u Nišu.

Voditelj projekta: Aleksandar Bulatović

Istraživanja o okolini Bora projektnog partnera Aleksandra Kapurana, Arheološki institut Beograd, u toku 2019. godine podržana su od strane Ministarstva kulture i informacija Republike Srbije.

Partners of Visualizing the Unknown Balkans / Partneri projekta Vizualizacija nepoznatog Balkana

(in alphabetical order / po abecednom redu)

Institute of Archaeology Belgrade
Aleksandar Bulatović and Aleksandar Kapuran
Kneza Mihaila 35
11000 Belgrade
Serbia

Museum of Mining and Metallurgy
Igor Jovanović
Moše Pijade 19
19210 Bor
Serbia

Semberija Museum
Snježana Antić
Karađorđeva 2
76300 Bijeljina
Bosnia and Herzegovina

National Museum Leskovac
Vladimir Stevanović
Stojana Ljubića 2
16000 Leskovac
Serbia

Museum of the City of Zenica
Ikbal Cogo
Muhameda Seida Serdarevića bb
72000 Zenica
Bosnia and Herzegovina

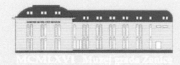

Acknowledgements / Zahvale

Serbian and Bosnian authorities

Serbian Ministry of Culture and Heritage

Institute of Archaeology in Belgrade

University of Belgrade, Laboratory for Bioarchaeology

National Museum in Leskovac

Austrian Embassy in Belgrade

Austrian Embassy in Sarajevo

Museum of Mining and Metallurgy in Bor

Museum of Semberija in Bijeljina

Museum of City of Zenica

Cultural art society (KUD) Gradina, Gradišće

Ambassador Nikolaus Lutterotti and Sabine Kroissenbrunner, Austrian Embassy, Belgrade

Minister Spahija Kozlić, Ministry of Education, Culture, Science and Sport of Zenica-Doboj Canton, Bosnia and Herzegovina

Armed Forces of Bosnia and Herzegovina and Colonel Robert Gašić

Momčilo Koprivica, director of Museum of Semberija, Bijeljina

Adnadin Jašarević, director of Museum of City of Zenica

Slaviša Perić for his scientific advice, Institute of Archaeology, Belgrade

Vujadin Ivanišević for his support and the provided LIDAR data for Svinjarička Čuka

Mathias Mehofer, VIAS, University of Vienna

Edin Bujak, University of Sarajevo

Stjepan Ćorić, Geologische Bundesanstalt, Vienna

Cornelius Meyer, Eastern Atlas, Berlin

Steffen Schneider, Marlen Schlöffel and team, Osnabrück University

Excavations teams / Učesnici iskopavanja

Svinjarička Čuka: Barbara Horejs, Aleksandar Bulatović, Bogdana Milić, Clare Burke, Michael Brandl, Felix Ostmann, Ognjen Mladenović, Vladimir Stevanović, Mario Börner, David Blattner, Dominik Bochatz, Laura Burkhardt, Mohamad Mustafa, Dragana Filipović, Jelena Bulatović, Amalia Sabanov, Dragana Perovanović, Nevena Pantić, Anastasija Stojanović

Thanks to Thomas Urban for database and Milivoje Milenković and Suzana Jovanović for hosting our team / Zahvaljemo Thomasu Urbanu za izradu baze podataka te Milivoju Milenkoviću i Suzani Jovanović za iskazano gostoprimstvo.

Bor: Mario Gavranović, Aleksandar Kapuran, Thomas Urban, Irene Petschko, Igor Jovanović, Mathias Mehofer, Nicole Mittermair, Marija Jovičić, Marina Dević, Francesco Bisaccia, Michael Konrad, Novica Dragojević

Zenica: Mario Gavranović, Edin Bujak, Ikbal Cogo, Mustafa Uzunalić, Nejla Burko, Samra Terzić, Irhad Škoro, Thomas Urban, Irene Petschko, Nicole Mittermair, Verena Tiedtke, Adem Dedić, Emir Karić

Bijeljina: Mario Gavranović, Snježana Antić, Mario Börner, Michael Konrad, Marlon Bas, Lukas Waltenberger

We thank all the workers who participated in the excavations / Zahvaljujemo se svim radnicima koji su učestvovali na iskopavanju.

Authors / Autori

(in alphabetical order / po abecednom redu)

Snježana Antić
Semberija Museum
Karađorđeva 2
76300 Bijeljina, Bosnia and Herzegovina
snjezanaa@gmail.com

Michael Brandl
Institute for Oriental and European Archaeology
Austrian Academy of Sciences
Hollandstraße 11–13
1020 Vienna, Austria
michael.brandl@oeaw.ac.at

Aleksandar Bulatović
Institute of Archaeology, Belgrade
Kneza Mihaila 35/IV
11000 Belgrade, Serbia
abulatovic3@gmail.com

Clare Burke
Institute for Oriental and European Archaeology
Austrian Academy of Sciences
Hollandstraße 11–13
1020 Vienna, Austria
clare.burke@oeaw.ac.at

Mario Gavranović
Institute for Oriental and European Archaeology
Austrian Academy of Sciences
Hollandstraße 11–13
1020 Vienna, Austria
mario.gavranovic@oeaw.ac.at

Barbara Horejs
Institute for Oriental and European Archaeology
Austrian Academy of Sciences
Hollandstraße 11–13
1020 Vienna, Austria
barbara.horejs@oeaw.ac.at

Aleksandar Kapuran
Institute of Archaeology, Belgrade
Kneza Mihaila 35/IV
11000 Belgrade, Serbia
a.kapuran@gmail.com

Mathias Mehofer
Vienna Institute for Archaeological Science VIAS
University of Vienna
Franz Klein-Gasse 1
1190 Vienna, Austria
mathias.mehofer@univie.ac.at

Bogdana Milić
Institute for Oriental and European Archaeology
Austrian Academy of Sciences
Hollandstraße 11–13
1020 Vienna, Austria
bogdana.milic@oeaw.ac.at

Irene M. Petschko
Institute for Oriental and European Archaeology
Austrian Academy of Sciences
Hollandstraße 11–13
1020 Vienna, Austria
irene.petschko@oeaw.ac.at

Lukas Waltenberger
Institute for Oriental and European Archaeology
Austrian Academy of Sciences
Hollandstraße 11–13
1020 Vienna, Austria
lukas.waltenberger@oeaw.ac.at